Japan's Remilitarisation

Christopher W. Hughes

Japan's Remilitarisation

Christopher W. Hughes

IISS The International Institute for Strategic Studies

The International Institute for Strategic Studies
Arundel House | 13–15 Arundel Street | Temple Place | London | WC2R 3DX | UK

First published April 2009 by **Routledge**
4 Park Square, Milton Park, Abingdon, Oxon, OX14 4RN

for **The International Institute for Strategic Studies**
Arundel House, 13–15 Arundel Street, Temple Place, London, WC2R 3DX, UK
www.iiss.org

Simultaneously published in the USA and Canada by **Routledge**
270 Madison Ave., New York, NY 10016

Routledge is an imprint of Taylor & Francis, an Informa Business

DIRECTOR-GENERAL AND CHIEF EXECUTIVE John Chipman
EDITOR Tim Huxley
MANAGER FOR EDITORIAL SERVICES Ayse Abdullah
COPYEDITOR Matthew Foley
ASSISTANT EDITOR Katharine Fletcher
COVER/PRODUCTION John Buck

The International Institute for Strategic Studies is an independent centre for research, information and debate on the problems of conflict, however caused, that have, or potentially have, an important military content. The Council and Staff of the Institute are international and its membership is drawn from almost 100 countries. The Institute is independent and it alone decides what activities to conduct. It owes no allegiance to any government, any group of governments or any political or other organisation. The IISS stresses rigorous research with a forward-looking policy orientation and places particular emphasis on bringing new perspectives to the strategic debate.

The Institute's publications are designed to meet the needs of a wider audience than its own membership and are available on subscription, by mail order and in good bookshops. Further details at www.iiss.org.

Printed and bound in Great Britain by Bell & Bain Ltd, Thornliebank, Glasgow

British Library Cataloguing in Publication Data
A catalogue record for this book is available from the British Library

Library of Congress Cataloging in Publication Data

ISBN 978-0-415-55692-7
ISSN 0567-932X

ADELPHI 403

Contents

GLOSSARY

ADF	Australian Defence Force
APEC	Asia-Pacific Economic Cooperation (Forum)
ASDF	Air Self Defense Force
ATD-X	Advanced Technology Demonstration-X
ATSML	Anti-Terrorism Special Measures Law
AWACS	Airborne Warning and Control System
BADGE	Base Air Defense Ground Environment
BJOCC	Bilateral Joint Operations Coordination Center
BMD	ballistic-missile defence
CENTCOM	Central Command
CRG	Central Readiness Group
CRIO	Cabinet Intelligence Research Office
CSICE	Cabinet Satellite Intelligence Center
CSIS	Center for Strategic and International Studies
CTF	Combined Task Force
DDH	Destroyer-Helicopter
DFAA	Defense Facilities Administration Agency
DPJ	Democratic Party of Japan
DPRI	Defense Policy Review Initiative
FHI	Fuji Heavy Industries
FMS	foreign military sales
GE	General Electric
GPR	Global Posture Review
GSDF	Ground Self Defense Force
GSMIA	General Security of Military Information Agreement
HNS	host-nation support
IAEA	International Atomic Energy Agency

ICBM	intercontinental ballistic missile
IED	improvised explosive device
IFSEC	US–Japan Industry Forum for Security Cooperation
IHI	Ishikawajima Harima Heavy Industries
IIPS	Institute for International Policy Studies
IPCL	International Peace Cooperation Law
ISAF	International Security Assistance Force
IGS	intelligence-gathering satellite
JADGE	Japan Air Defense Ground Environment
JADSC	Japan–Australia Joint Declaration on Security Cooperation
JCG	Japan Coast Guard
JDA	Japan Defense Agency
JDAM	joint direct attack munitions
JNSC	Japan National Security Council
JSC	Joint Staff Council
JSDF	Japan Self Defense Forces
JSO	Joint Staff Office
KHI	Kawasaki Heavy Industries
LDP	Liberal Democratic Party
MBT	main battle tank
MELCO	Mitsubishi Electric Company
METI	Ministry of Economy, Trade and Industry
MHI	Mitsubishi Heavy Industries
MOF	Ministry of Finance
MOFA	Ministry of Foreign Affairs
MSA	Maritime Safety Agency
MSDF	Maritime Self Defense Force
MTDP	Mid-Term Defense Programme
NBC	nuclear, biological and chemical
NDPG	National Defense Programme Guidelines
NDPO	National Defense Programme Outline
NIDS	National Institute of Defense Studies
NPA	National Police Agency
NPR	National Police Reserve
NPT	Nuclear Non-Proliferation Treaty
NSF	National Safety Force

NSG	Nuclear Suppliers Group
NSRG	Congressional National Security Research Group
ODA	official development assistance
OEF	*Operation Enduring Freedom*
PAC-3	*Patriot* Advanced Capability-3
PKO	peacekeeping operation
PLAN	People's Liberation Army Navy
PLH	patrol large helicopter
PRC	Policy Research Council
PSI	Proliferation Security Initiative
PRT	Provincial Reconstruction Team
PT	Project Team
RSSML	Replenishment Support Special Measures Law
SACO	Special Action Committee on Okinawa
SAR	synthetic-aperture radar
SBU	Special Boarding Unit
SCC	Security Consultative Committee
SDPJ	Social Democratic Party of Japan
SHDOS	Strategic Headquarters for the Development of Outer Space
SLOC	sea lines of communication
SM-3 BLK IA	Standard Missile-3 Block IA
SM-3 BLK IIA	Standard Missile-3 Block IIA
SOFA	Status of Forces Agreement
SOG	Special Operations Group
SST	Special Security Team
TRDI	Technical Research and Development Institute
TSD	Trilateral Security Dialogue
UAV	unmanned aerial vehicle
UNMIN	UN Political Mission in Nepal
UNMIS	UN Mission in Sudan
UNPKO	UN peacekeeping operations
USAF	US Air Force
WMD	weapons of mass destruction

INTRODUCTION

Japan embarked upon a rapid, even radical, development of its security policy under the administration of Prime Minister Junichiro Koizumi between April 2001 and September 2006. Japan also responded proactively to the 11 September attacks and the 'war on terror', passing an Anti-Terrorism Special Measures Law (ATSML) and dispatching the Maritime Self Defense Force (MSDF) from November 2001 onwards to provide logistical support in the Indian Ocean for US and international coalition forces engaged in *Operation Enduring Freedom*. In Iraq and Kuwait, the Ground Self Defense Force (GSDF) and Air Self Defense Force (ASDF) were deployed from 2004 under the Iraqi Reconstruction Law on non-combat reconstruction missions as part of the US-led 'coalition of the willing'. Koizumi's administration also set in train a series of initiatives to strengthen the Japan Self Defense Forces (JSDF) and extend the scope and functions of the US–Japan alliance. Japan's revised National Defense Programme Guidelines (NDPG) and Mid-Term Defense Programme (MTDP) of 2004 began the process of converting the JSDF into a more mobile military geared towards regional and global deployments.

Japan committed itself to bilateral technological and strategic cooperation on ballistic-missile defence (BMD) with the US, possibly to a greater extent than any other ally. Japan and the US concluded the Defense Policy Review Initiative (DPRI) in 2006, facilitating the realignment of US bases in Japan, promoting the greater integration of US and Japanese military forces and enabling the US to utilise its bases in Japan for global security functions. Because of these changes, Japan was seen to be moving towards the increased militarisation of its security stance, and to be emerging as a more assertive, 'normal' military power and reliable US ally.[1]

Following Koizumi's departure from the premiership in September 2006, his immediate successor, Shinzo Abe, appeared set to take Japanese security policy in yet more radical directions. Abe unveiled plans for a US-style Japan National Security Council (JNSC) to replace the existing more cumbersome Security Council of Japan, and proposed investigating ways to circumvent Japan's self-imposed ban on the exercise of the right of collective self-defence, revise Article 9 of the constitution and forge closer military links with the US, Australia, India and NATO, with the implicit intention of responding to China's rise. Under Abe's administration, Japanese policymakers even reacted to the North Korean nuclear test in October 2006 by attempting to start a debate on Japan's own nuclear options. Abe's plans for a more assertive Japan on a more equal footing with the US were, however, derailed when his governing Liberal Democratic Party (LDP) was heavily defeated in elections in July 2007, turning over control of the House of Councillors (the upper chamber of the Japanese parliament, the National Diet) to the main opposition Democratic Party of Japan (DPJ). The DPJ sought to block renewal of the ATSML extending the MSDF's mission in the Indian Ocean, triggering Abe's political downfall in

September 2007. Two months later, in November 2007, the MSDF was forced to withdraw from the Indian Ocean and return to Japan.

Abe's successor, Prime Minister Yasuo Fukuda, proved much more cautious on security policy. Although Fukuda did succeed in passing a new Replenishment Support Special Measures Law (RSSML) enabling the MSDF's redeployment to support *Operation Enduring Freedom* in January 2008, thereby keeping his pledge to then US President George W. Bush to maintain a Japanese presence in the Indian Ocean, he was forced to rely on the extraordinary measure of using the LDP's two-thirds 'super-majority' in the House of Representatives lower chamber to override DPJ opposition in the upper chamber. To placate the LDP's dovish coalition partner New Komeito, Fukuda also scaled back Japan's military activities in support of the international coalition, restricting them to refuelling and the supply of water. Fukuda's precarious domestic political situation meant that he was equally hesitant in other areas of security cooperation, shelving plans for a JNSC and backing away from an investigation into the ban on collective self-defence. Fukuda's premiership was also beset with a series of scandals connected with the Ministry of Defense and the JSDF, involving corrupt military procurement practices, potential leaks of military information and failures of civilian control. The impression of scandal was compounded in February 2007, when a Japanese *Aegis* destroyer failed to follow safety procedures and collided with a civilian fishing vessel off the Japanese coast, killing the two-man crew. These scandals inflicted severe damage on the reputation of the Japanese military establishment and complicated the political debate on Japan's future military stance.

Fukuda's main preoccupation thus became to control these scandals, and his eventual fall from power in September 2008, much as with Abe's, was the result of domestic political failures compounded by travails over security policy. In mid 2008, he toyed with introducing a new permanent dispatch law (*kokyu hoan*) for JSDF international security cooperation, so as to obviate the need for separate time-bound laws and for extensive National Diet debates over each overseas deployment, and to enable the GSDF and ASDF to fulfil non-combat logistical and reconstruction missions in Afghanistan. Fukuda was frustrated in this endeavour, however, in part by the DPJ, but also by opposition from within the LDP itself and from New Komeito, and by public opposition, all of which were aware of the risks of involvement on the ground in Afghanistan. By late 2008, Fukuda had realised that the DPJ would again block the renewal of the RSSML and demonstrate the inability of his administration to maintain its most public promises of international security cooperation.

Fukuda's replacement, Taro Aso, has so far proved bolder than his predecessor, forcing through the renewal of the RSSML in December 2008 and ordering the dispatch of the MSDF in March 2009 to participate in new international anti-piracy missions off Somalia. However, Aso's attempts to maintain a more proactive security stance face similar problems to his predecessors'; his position as prime minister looks uncertain amid domestic political and economic problems, and his freedom of action in security affairs remains constrained by New Komeito and the DPJ.

Radicalism or retrenchment in Japan's security policy?

Has Japan's security policy become moribund after Koizumi's audacious premiership, or is Japan still set on strengthening its military stance, despite changes in political leadership? To some observers, Japan appears to be reasserting its traditional preference for a low-profile defence posture and highly limited alliance arrangements with the US, seemingly confirming the view that strong, even immovable, internal resistance makes deeper security commitments impossible.[2] Koizumi's tenure, and the significant remilitarisation of Japanese security that occurred during it, are seen as a short-term aberration. For others, Japan is continuing to slice away at its post-war military constraints. In this view, the caution of Koizumi's successors will prove untenable as Japan faces growing international pressures to adopt a more active security role.[3]

The objective of this book is to engage in the debate on Japan's post-Koizumi security stance. In particular, it seeks to gauge whether Japan has retrenched its military posture, or whether it has continued on the more radical path evident since 2001. It complements and builds on an earlier Adelphi Paper which covered the period up to mid 2004, updating and adjusting the analysis to take account of the last five years, and looking ahead to future changes in Japan's security policy.[4] The book analyses the developments in security policy just outlined, including the Koizumi legacy, security planning under Abe, Fukuda and Aso, fluctuations in US–Japan alliance ties, and defence-related scandals. It also seeks to place these issues within wider, longer-term trends in Japan's defence capabilities, US–Japan alliance cooperation and domestic debates on Japan's security policy.

This is an opportune time to re-examine Japan's security trajectory in light of the preparation of a revised NDPG and MTDP for release in 2009; the implementation of a series of key Ministry of Defense and JSDF reforms from 2009 onwards; and the transition from the Bush era to the Barack Obama presidency in the US, bringing with it new expectations for the US–Japan alliance, and during which the two countries will mark the 50th anniversary of the revision in 1960 of the Treaty of Mutual Cooperation and Security Between the United States and Japan. All of these developments will contribute to consolidating existing trends, setting a new long-term agenda for Japan's security policy.

In order to provide context and a means to gauge short-term versus long-term changes in Japan's security policy and military stance, this book focuses on several key aspects of security policy. All of these areas – defence expenditure, the size and power-projection capabilities of the armed forces, civil–military relations, military-industrial complexes, external military and alliance commitments and domestic institutional and normative military constraints – are 'classic' indicators for calibrating the degree of long-term structural change in any state's security policy.[5] However, they are especially pertinent to Japan because, in all cases, they constitute self-imposed and self-declaratory standards.[6] Hence, if it can be shown – and this book argues that it can – that Japan has progressively eroded or breached its own constraints, a clear picture can be established of Japan's long-term remilitarisation.

Chapter 1 provides an overview of the characteristics and evolution of Japan's security policy in the post-war period, in order to provide the essential baselines for judging the extent of its remilitarisation during and after the Koizumi administration. The chapter discusses the range of regional and global security challenges facing Japan, which have propelled it along its more proactive military path.

Chapter 2 investigates the first specific, long-term indicator of Japan's move to a remilitarised security stance by revealing changes in Japanese defence expenditure and JSDF capabilities. The chapter uses a range of information, including statistics relating to deferred payments and the 'paramilitary' Japan Coast Guard (JCG) unavailable in previous studies, to demonstrate that the defence budget does not represent an absolute or immutable constraint on Japanese procurement programmes. In contrast to recent short-term speculation about retrenchment in Japanese security planning, this chapter presents long-term evidence of proactive trends in JSDF procurement, for five or ten years hence, which indicate growing power-projection capabilities, and consequently evolving options to expand participation in US-led multinational and UN operations in East Asia and globally.

Chapter 3 turns to civilian control in Japan and its durability as a prime constraint on Japanese military ambitions. It demonstrates that traditional civilian control structures have been eroding over the last decade, a process accelerated under Koizumi, and continuing apace under his successors. It focuses on a set of defence-related scandals as manifestations of longer-term trends in the erosion of civilian control. The chapter considers how Ministry of Defense and JSDF reform efforts are creating the long-term foundation Japan needs to implement a potentially even more proactive security policy.

Chapter 4 gauges long-term structural change in Japan's security policy by considering the emergence of domestic and international 'military-industrial complexes'. The chapter examines Japan's changing defence production and the impetus it is creating for structural collusion between political, bureaucratic, military and industrial interests and the effects on procurement decisions. It also considers how Japan's changing defence production is creating transnational linkages with US industry that help tighten US–Japan alliance ties and contribute to breaches of the ban on arms exports – two new key manifestations of external militarisation.

Chapter 5 examines Japan's overseas military engagements in the form of the deployment of military forces through the developing mechanisms of the US–Japan alliance and participation in UN-centred military activities. Just as importantly, Japan's commitments are considered in terms of support for US power projection from Japanese bases for operations in

East Asia, the Middle East and beyond. This is because, all too often, Japan's remilitarisation is assessed in terms of a false dichotomy – moves to independently deploy the JSDF overseas versus the alleged constraints of the US–Japan alliance on Japanese military ambitions. Simultaneously, observers have tended to neglect Japan's significant security role in providing bases which help to underwrite, physically and financially, the global US military presence. It is vital to understand that Japan's support for the infrastructure of US global military power is an extension of its own remilitarisation.

The chapter looks at post-Koizumi developments in US–Japan security cooperation, and shows how far domestic political tensions have induced Japan to pull back from alliance commitments. It argues that, since Koizumi, there has been some scaling back of more ambitious US–Japan alliance cooperation beyond East Asia, and there have been problems in implementing elements of the DPRI, the realignment of bases in Okinawa and shocks to alliance confidence over responses to North Korea's nuclearisation. However, it is also argued that alliance ties remain strong, and that the most significant elements of the DPRI, including the co-location of US and Japanese command and control systems and the US use of its bases in Japan to project power beyond the Asia-Pacific, are proceeding regardless of current political debates. In addition, the chapter considers Japan's search for new means to expand external military commitments. It explores the ways in which Japanese policymakers have made special efforts, often in the face of domestic opposition, to forge new security ties with Australia and India, to consider deployment to Afghanistan and to dispatch the JSDF on new anti-piracy missions in the Gulf of Aden.

Chapter 6 analyses long-term changes in the key domestic institutional and normative constraints on Japan's military stance. The chapter investigates the strengthened legitimacy of the JSDF in the eyes of the public; a new propensity to debate transgressing Japan's non-nuclear principles; current and long-term trends in moves towards revision and reinterpretation of Article 9 of the so-called 'Peace Constitution'; and Japanese public attitudes towards military and patriotic education and the use of armed force for national security ends. It demonstrates that, in all of these areas, Japanese resistance to an enhanced societal status for the JSDF and the efficacy of military power is being eroded, creating in turn a new long-term basis of support for Japan's wider international security ambitions.

Japan's regional and global significance

Taken together, this book presents a set of comprehensive and objective indicators which point towards Japan's continuing remilitarisation. It provides evidence that Japan's security policy is undergoing long-term structural change, predisposing it towards a more assertive military stance, and that domestic political machinations have not halted this process. In fact, the formulation of much of Japan's security policy remains insulated from political fluctuations, and many security-related issues believed to have impeded a more assertive security stance – such as defence procurement and defence-related scandals – are actually manifestations of ongoing structural change, creating the basis for further reform and potentially greater dynamism.

Japan's continuing remilitarisation has important ramifications for international security. The use here of the term 'remilitarisation' should not be read as an alarmist warning that Japan is necessarily intent on reverting to the kind of state it became between 1931 and 1945. Japan remains a constrained military actor, reluctant to pursue the full potential panoply of national military capabilities, limited by its junior alliance relationship with the US and its strong residual anti-militaristic sentiment. Nevertheless, it has to be acknowledged that Japan, judged by the objective international yardstick of the key indicators of remilitarisation, which in turn are Japan's own benchmarks, is set upon a long-term trajectory that will see it assuming a more assertive regional and global security role. Japan can certainly in no way be said to be demilitarising or to have reached stasis in its security policy. All the long-term indications point to activism and expansion in its military capabilities and international commitments.

Such expansion clearly affects the East Asian power balance; indeed, in some respects Japan is engaged in a low-key arms race with China, and is hedging its nuclear stance vis-à-vis North Korea. Japan's attempts to enhance security ties with Australia, South Korea and India also impact upon the regional security landscape. Just as crucial, though, is Japan's approach to its alliance with the US. Japan's increasing support for, and participation in, US regional power projection holds the key to Washington's attempts to deter a nuclearising North Korea and a rising China. Similarly, the expanding functional and geographical scope of US–Japan alliance cooperation increasingly holds the key to efforts by US administrations to maintain their state's global military hegemony. This logic is likely to induce Obama's administration and its Japanese counterparts to keep pushing ever outwards the envelope of bilateral military cooperation.

CHAPTER ONE

The Trajectory of Japan's Remilitarisation

Japan has demonstrated the features of both a militarised and a demilitarised state. This chapter provides an overview of Japan's security policy and military posture from the aftermath of the Second World War to the contemporary period, with a particular focus on developments over the last decade or so in order to provide the necessary context and benchmarks for evaluating the extent of remilitarisation under Koizumi and his successors. It outlines the strategic challenges underlying the short-term inertia in Japan's security policy, and the strategic imperatives pressing for continuing and longer-term change in the key indicators of remilitarisation considered in the subsequent chapters.

Japan's post-war remilitarisation

In the pre-war period, Japan maintained a powerful military establishment, with a high level of military spending, mass conscription and a paramilitary force (the *Kempeitai* military police) under the partial direction of the powerful Home Ministry (the *Naimusho*). Progressively removed from civilian control, the military assumed increasing influence over the top political leadership, and a growing, if at times uncoordinated, military-industrial complex emerged.[1] Japan was also deeply immersed in the 'militarism of the mind', with a body politic centred on the emperor system and nationalistic and militaristic education.[2]

In the immediate post-war period, during the early phases of the Allied Occupation, Japan was pulled to the other extreme, becoming a fully demilitarised state. The Imperial Army and Navy were disbanded, the defence-production industry was broken up and the militarism of the pre-war period was rejected in the country's new, post-war constitution.[3] The Preamble of the constitution states Japanese ideals with regard to security:

> We, the Japanese people, desire peace for all time and are deeply conscious of the high ideals controlling human relationships, and we have determined to preserve our security and existence, trusting in the justice and faith of the peace-loving peoples of the world. We desire to occupy an honoured place in an international society striving for the preservation of peace, and the banishment of tyranny and slavery, oppression and intolerance for all time from the earth. We recognise that all peoples of the world have the right to live in peace, free from fear and want.

Chapter 2, Article 9, 'The Renunciation of War', reads as follows:

> Aspiring sincerely to an international peace based on justice and order, the Japanese people forever renounce war as a sovereign right of the nation and the threat or use of force as means of settling international disputes.

> In order to accomplish the aim of the preceding paragraph, land, sea, and air forces, as well as other war potential, will never be maintained. The right of belligerency of the state will not be recognised.

However, with the onset of the Cold War, Japan began to move away from this highly demilitarised stance. Japan's programme of demilitarisation and democratisation halted as policymakers and the US-led occupying powers focused on reinforcing Japan's position as a bastion of anti-communism in the Far East. Japanese policymakers originally interpreted Article 9 as prohibiting both offensive war and the right of national self-defence, but from the 1950s onwards they have held to an interpretation allowing Japan, in line with its position as a sovereign state under the UN Charter, to exercise the right of individual self-defence (*kobetsu-teki jieiken*), and to maintain military capabilities for this purpose.[4] (This is in line with an amendment made in the National Diet before the article's promulgation which led to the insertion of the phrase 'in order to accomplish the aim of the preceding paragraph', thus opening the way for the interpretation of Japan maintaining military forces as long as these were not designed for the settling of international disputes.) Hence, Japanese leaders, encouraged by the US, moved to rearm within the limits of national economic capacity, with the formation in 1950 and 1952 respectively, of the National Police Reserve (NPR) and National Safety Force (NSF), the forerunners of the JSDF, which was established in 1955. The bilateral US–Japan security treaty was signed in 1951. This was a 'grand strategic bargain' under which Japan accepted alignment with and security guarantees from the US in return for the provision of bases from which the US could project power onto the East Asian continent.[5] Japan also accepted that the price of the security treaty was to conclude only a 'partial peace' solely with the US and its aligned states, excluding the Soviet Union and China. A peace treaty with China was not signed until 1978, and no treaty was ever concluded with the Soviet Union (nor with its successor state, Russia).

For the remainder of the Cold War, gradual remilitarisation continued through the incremental building up of the JSDF's quantitative and qualitative capabilities and closer military cooperation between Japan and the US, to the point that, by 1981, Prime Minister Zenko Suzuki was able for the first time to publicly refer to US–Japan security arrangements as an 'alliance'. Japan and the US developed a relatively robust division of labour in security during the latter stages of the Cold War in order to deter the Soviet Union in the Far East. Under this arrangement, the JSDF defended Japan's own territory and the surrounding sea and airspace, providing an effective 'shield' for US deployments in Japan and to complement the US 'sword' of offensive power projection in East Asia.

Japan consolidated its military posture through the 1976 National Defense Programme Outline (NDPO), the country's first attempt to set out the principles of its military doctrine and the force structure necessary to implement it. The NDPO was notable in stressing not only the need to build up the JSDF, but also that Japan would maintain forces designed to repel aggression in the first instance, and would seek US support if this proved impossible, thus developing a military doctrine predicated upon the closer coordination of US and Japanese forces. Japan further strengthened its coordination with the US through the 1978 Guidelines for US–Japan Defense Cooperation, which outlined for the first time areas for bilateral cooperation relating to Japan's immediate defence under Article 5 of the security treaty (including tactical planning, joint exercises and logistical support), and for cooperation in regional contingencies in the Far East under Article 6.

Nevertheless, even as Japanese remilitarisation advanced it was subject to significant brakes, because Japanese policymakers feared the costs of entanglement in the Cold War and US regional and global military strategy. Policymakers erected a number of domestic barriers to remilitarisation. Japan held strongly to its policy of an exclusively defensive posture (*senshu boei*), founded upon its adherence to the right of individual self-defence and reinforced by a number of constitutional prohibitions and anti-militaristic principles. Most famously, the size of the JSDF was limited by imposing a ceiling of 1% of gross national product (GNP) on defence expenditures in 1976, and the range of its capabilities was constrained by prohibitions preventing the acquisition of weapons that were overtly offensive in nature. In practice, this has meant that the JSDF does not possess power-projection capabilities, including intercontinental ballistic missiles (ICBMs), long-range strike aircraft and 'offensive' aircraft carriers.[6] The National Diet further constrained military capabilities by passing a resolution in 1969 restricting Japanese activities in space to peaceful purposes (*heiwa no mokuteki ni kagiri*).

Japan also imposed rigid civilian controls over the JSDF, and restricted the growth of a military-industrial complex by subordinating domestic military industry to the civilian sector. Meanwhile, a determination to maximise national autonomy by maintaining an indigenous defence-production base meant that defence-industrial cooperation with the US was limited. Bans were imposed on the export of weapons technology in 1967 and 1976, preventing Japan from exporting arms and becoming involved in the militarisation efforts of other states; Japan remained reluctant to dispatch troops overseas, and resisted open-ended commitments under its treaty obligations to the US.[7]

Alongside its interpretation of Article 9 as permitting individual self-defence, Japan maintained an additional interpretation prohibiting the exercise of the right of collective self-defence (*shudan-teki jieiken*). Japan's government recognises that, as a sovereign state, it possesses the inherent right of collective self-defence under Chapter 7 of the UN Charter, but since 1954 has taken the position that the actual exercise of this right would exceed the minimum force necessary for the purposes of self-defence and would be unconstitutional. Japan's prohibition on the exercise of collective self-defence thus limited its external remilitarisation and ability to assist its US ally outside its own immediate territory.

Japan's policymakers also sought to minimise external alliance obligations by insisting that the use of US bases for overseas military operations required bilateral consultation, and that the geographical scope of the US–Japan security treaty was limited to the Far East. Military command structures remained fundamentally separate from those of the US, limiting the risk of becoming embroiled in US regional military actions. Moreover, Japan's policymakers showed a marked reluctance to conduct bilateral research on Article 6 contingencies, preferring instead to focus on the defence of Japan itself.

Finally, Japan's process of remilitarisation was arrested by the continuing strength of domestic institutions and anti-militarist norms, including public mistrust of the JSDF, adherence to the Three Non-Nuclear Principles (*hikaku sangensoku*: not to produce, possess or introduce nuclear weapons) enunciated in 1967, resistance to attempts to revise Article 9, and suspicion of the promotion of patriotic education and of the legitimacy of the use of force for national security ends. Indeed, Japan attempted in the post-war period to articulate alternative conceptions of comprehensive security, emphasising the use of diplomacy, economic engagement and official development assistance (ODA).

As has been noted elsewhere, and as outlined in more detail below, these brakes on remilitarisation certainly became less of a restraint during the Cold War period. The 1% of GNP ceiling on defence spending was first breached in 1986, the Three Non-Nuclear Principles were weakened with the introduction into and transit through Japanese ports of nuclear weapons on US ships, direct US–Japan military-industrial cooperation began in projects such as the co-development of the FS-X fighter, and US–Japan alliance cooperation expanded.[8] However, many observers were struck by Japan's stubbornly incremental approach to remilitarisation in this period, which rendered it still essentially a highly constrained military power by the end of the Cold War.[9]

Japan's new security environment

Japan's propensity to shift incrementally towards remilitarisation has been accentuated by changes in the regional and global security environment since the end of the Cold War. The most immediate regional security threat confronting Japan is North Korea. Japanese anxieties have focused on North Korea's development of nuclear weapons, demonstrated most graphically by the North's detonation of a nuclear device in October 2006. These anxieties have been compounded by the North's ballistic-missile programme, raising concerns that Japan could face attack by conventional missiles, or that Pyongyang may eventually master and miniaturise nuclear technologies so that its missiles could be used to deliver nuclear warheads. Japan's vulnerability to missile attack was demonstrated by the '*Taepo-dong-1* shock' in August 1998, when North Korea test-fired a missile over Japanese airspace, and again by the North's testing of ballistic missiles in the Sea of Japan in July 2006, although many of these missiles actually splashed down closer to Russia, China and North Korea itself. In March 2009, North Korea was believed to be preparing to launch a *Taepo-dong-2* missile into the Sea of Japan or Eastern Pacific area. Additionally, Japanese policymakers have been concerned about the incursion of North Korean 'spy ships' (*fushinsen*) on espionage missions, leading it to use force against the North's ships in March 1999 and December 2001, and are worried about possible guerrilla attacks on key facilities, such as nuclear-power installations on the Sea of Japan coastline.[10]

If North Korea represents the most immediate threat to Japan's security, then China poses the greatest challenge in the medium to long term. Japan has been concerned at China's modernisation of its conventional and nuclear forces since the early 1990s, in particular the lack of transparency in its double-digit increases in defence expenditure over the last decade.[11] Japan's military planners watch carefully the augmentation of China's ballistic- and cruise-missile capabilities, including new submarine-launched cruise missiles with a range of around 2,000 kilometres and with capabilities similar to US *Tomahawks*, and the general upgrading of its air-defence and offence capabilities through the deployment of Su-27 and Su-30MK strike aircraft, indigenously developed J-10 and FB-7A combat aircraft, a new J-X stealth fighter and the airborne and early warning and control (AWACS) KJ-2000 programme.[12] China's military ambitions in space are an additional concern. Japan was alarmed at China's test of an anti-satellite system in January 2007, which is probably capable of disrupting US satellite capabilities and Japan's burgeoning military satellite programme.[13]

Japan's concerns vis-à-vis China focus not just on its military build-up but also on signs that it is now willing to project military power beyond its borders in support of its national interests. Japan is aware that China could disrupt sea lanes with only a small blue-water surface, submarine and amphibious naval capacity and through the assertion of its territorial claims in the East China Sea and the Senkaku/Daioyu islets. Hence, Japan has viewed with some apprehension China's introduction of Type 052C *Luyang* II destroyers, Type 051C *Luzhou* destroyers and Type 054A *Jiangkai* frigates, which will provide capabilities similar to those of the *Aegis* air-defence system operated by the US and Japan. China also remains interested in aircraft-carrier technologies, demonstrated by its refurbishment of the former Ukrainian carrier *Varyag* in Dalian since 2002, and there is speculation that China might purchase Su-33 fighters from Russia modified for carrier use. Japan has also taken note of Chinese submarine incursions into its territorial waters: it detected the passage of a Chinese nuclear-powered submarine in its waters on 10 November 2004 (China apologised and claimed the vessel had unintentionally veered off course), and claimed that a Chinese submarine entered its territorial waters in September 2008 (which China denied). Tokyo has also taken note of China's decision in December 2008 to dispatch two destroyers for anti-piracy missions off Somalia, which has been taken as a sign of Beijing's global naval power-projection ambitions.

Bilateral ties between China and Japan have been further complicated by issues connected to Japan's colonial past, the status of Taiwan and Sino-US strategic competition. Japan viewed with alarm the Taiwan Strait crisis of 1995–96 and China's intimidation of Taiwan through the test-firing of ballistic missiles, seeing this as another indication of China's willingness to project military power in pursuit of its national interests, and possibly to challenge the US militarily in the region over the longer term – perhaps even striking at US forces in Japan in the event of a full-blown conflict resulting from any Taiwanese move to declare independence.

Japan's list of regional security concerns do not stop with North Korea and China. Security planners now have to contend with the emergence of Russia as a more assertive regional player. In February 2008, two Japanese F-15s were scrambled to intercept a Russian Tu-95 strategic bomber that had violated Japanese airspace at the end of the Izu island chain, some 650km south of Tokyo. Another two Tu-95s were reportedly intercepted in October 2008, prompting Russia to send two Su-27 fighters to the scene.[14] Russian railing against US missile-defence plans, and by implication Japan's cooperation with the US on ballistic-missile defence, has also been disconcerting. Meanwhile, mindful of its own territorial dispute with Russia over the Northern Territories, Japan watched with alarm Moscow's resort to force in its dispute with Georgia in August 2008. In response, Japan cancelled search-and-rescue exercises with the Russian Navy scheduled for September 2008, which would have involved Russian ships sharing Japanese ports with US vessels. Finally, South Korea has continued to increase its defence expenditure and to build up its blue-water naval capacity, notably in the shape of *Aegis* destroyers. Japanese policymakers are mindful that, despite South Korea's status as a fellow US ally, it is locked in dispute with Japan over the sovereignty of the Takeshima islets, often involving demonstrations of military force.

Developments outside its immediate region have also presented Japan with a new series of global security challenges that demand a new set of answers. Japan's response to the 1990–91 Gulf War – it underwrote the allied war effort financially to the tune of $13 billion, but refused to commit the JSDF – was criticised internationally, making Japanese policymakers aware for the first time of the need for a more active and direct stance in support of international efforts to address major post-Cold War security crises. In the wake of the 9/11 attacks, Japan became aware of the threat of transnational terrorism and felt the need to support the US-led coalition in its efforts to expunge this threat in Afghanistan and elsewhere. Japanese policymakers agree with their US counterparts on the need to halt the proliferation of weapons of mass destruction, and have demonstrated an awareness of the security threats posed by failing states and humanitarian crises in areas such as Darfur. The resurgence of maritime piracy in Southeast Asia and in the waters around Somalia is another source of concern.

Japan's response to regional and global challenges

Japan's preferred role in responding to this security agenda has been non-military, relying on economic power and diplomacy. Tokyo has continued to search for means to engage North Korea diplomatically on nuclear and missile issues, as well as on its particular concerns over past abductions of Japanese citizens. Koizumi visited North Korea in September 2002 and May 2004, and Japan has provided important support to the Six-Party Talks process.

Similarly, Japan has sought to engage China. Since 2006, Koizumi's successors have attempted to forge a 'Mutually Beneficial Relationship Based on Common Strategic Interests', covering cooperation in politics, economics, development, energy and security. Japan accepted the first-ever visit by a Chinese destroyer to its ports in November 2007, and reciprocated by sending a destroyer to China in June 2008, carrying relief supplies for earthquake victims in Sichuan. Japan and China also discussed using ASDF aircraft to transport relief supplies, but public opposition to what would have been the first Japanese military presence in the Chinese interior since the 1940s put paid to the plan. Meanwhile, Japan has where possible sought to construct a strategic partnership with Russia and improve bilateral defence exchanges, and has considered ways to deepen military cooperation with South Korea.

Alongside these diplomatic efforts, however, Japan has also increasingly accepted the need to bolster its military capacity to respond to regional and global threats. In particular, Japanese policymakers are aware that the US–Japan alliance, the essential foundation of Japan's security policy in the post-war period, risks coming undone if Japan is not seen to be making greater efforts to support its ally. The potential vulnerability of the alliance first became clear during the North Korean nuclear crisis of 1994–95, when the US asked Japan for active support in the event of a conflict on the Korean Peninsula, including rear-area logistical support. Japanese policymakers were unable to respond effectively, revealing the alliance's lack of military operability, prompting a crisis of political confidence in the bilateral relationship with the US, and raising the prospect of Japan's abandonment by the US as an unreliable ally. Japan's alliance travails were exacerbated by tensions connected with US bases in Okinawa, mainly over the costs of supporting this presence, but also linked to crimes by US service personnel, military accidents and environmental pollution.

From the mid 1990s onwards, Japanese policymakers concluded that, to respond to emerging regional security challenges and new demands from the US for regional and global security cooperation, they needed to reformulate national defence doctrines and JSDF capabilities, and to redefine certain aspects of the US–Japan alliance. In June 1992, Japan passed an International Peace Cooperation Law (IPCL) to enable JSDF forces to participate in non-combat peacekeeping operations mounted by the UN. The JSDF has subsequently taken part in UN peacekeeping operations (UNPKO) in Cambodia (1992–93), Mozambique (1993–95), Rwanda (1994), the Golan Heights (from 1996) and Timor Leste (2002–04). In 2002, Japan 'unfroze' provisions in the IPCL allowing the JSDF to participate in a wider range of UN missions, including the monitoring of cease-fires, weapons collection and prisoner exchanges.

More significantly, in November 1995 Japan issued a revised NDPO. This stressed the need for stronger US–Japan alliance cooperation and contained a new clause stating that, should an adverse situation arise in areas surrounding Japan (*shuhen*) that impacted upon national peace and security, Japan should seek to deal with it in cooperation with the UN and within US–Japan security arrangements. Japan and the US then issued a 'Joint Declaration on Security' in April 1996 that opened the way for a revision of the US–Japan Guidelines for Defense Cooperation. In 1997 the revised guidelines specified for the first time the extent of Japanese logistical support for the US in the event of a regional contingency (*shuhen jitai*), thereby beginning a process of switching the emphasis of alliance cooperation from Article 5 to Article 6 of the security treaty. Finally, in 2001 and 2004, Japan provided non-combat logistical and reconstruction support to the US-led coalitions in Afghanistan and Iraq.

Since the end of Koizumi's administration in 2006, signs of caution and even retrenchment have become evident, in line with domestic political changes. However, Japan faces the same fundamental security pressures, and these will entail continued, if less dramatic, remilitarisation. In particular, demands from the US have continued for Japan to upgrade its military capabilities and the US–Japan alliance to enhance its ability to respond to global contingencies. Japanese policymakers are aware that the US has sought to activate its regional alliances in support of global security. The US has stressed a move away from 'threat-based' regional alliances to 'capabilities-based' global ones, with the capacity to construct flexible coalitions with interoperable military assets suited to the 'arc of instability' stretching from the Middle East to Southeast Asia. In addition, the Global Posture Review (GPR) of 2004 made clear the US intention that bases provided by regional alliances should be integrated into its strategy for the 'surging' and global deployment of its forward forces.[15] Under Koizumi and his successors, Japan has been forced to contemplate long-term responses to this emerging US military agenda. Although the exact military priorities of the Obama administration were still emerging in early 2009, Tokyo is likely to receive little respite from US demands for a more global security role within the alliance. Japan is thus engaged in a long-term process of shaping its security policy and defence capabilities such that it can provide for its own national defence and support US–Japan alliance cooperation.

Conclusion

Over the last decade and a half, Japan has faced growing, indeed near relentless, demands from a series of regional and global crises, from its US ally and from domestic constituencies to contribute more actively to international military affairs. It has responded by seeking an expanded regional and global military role involving the increased use of the JSDF overseas and the enhancement of US–Japan bilateral military cooperation. The succeeding chapters analyse the impact of these pressures on Japan's long-term remilitarisation, in terms of evolving military capabilities, civilian control, defence production, US–Japan alliance cooperation and societal attitudes towards the military and the use of force.

CHAPTER TWO

Japan's Military Doctrine, Expenditure and Power Projection

Japan's changing defence doctrines and capabilities

In order to respond to the multifarious security challenges it faces, Japan has found it necessary to embark upon successive revisions of its national defence doctrines and capabilities. This process, initiated towards the end of Koizumi's administration, has continued under his successors. Japan released a revised NDPG in December 2004, together with a new MTDP for 2005–09 setting out the country's long-term military procurement plans. The NDPG followed the 1995 NDPO in stressing Japan's regional security concerns and the importance of the US–Japan alliance in responding to them, but moved beyond its predecessor by outlining a range of new threats, including ballistic-missile strikes, guerrilla and special-operations attacks, incursions into its territorial waters and chemical and biological warfare. These concerns are a clear reflection of North Korean and Chinese activities; indeed, the NDPG went further than the 1995 NDPO, not only in identifying North Korea specifically as a destabilising factor in East Asia, but also for the first time highlighting concerns about China's impact on regional security, albeit in oblique terms (Japan, the document said, would 'remain attentive' to China's future military modernisation).[1] The NDPG also went beyond the 1995 NDPO in its emphasis on global security interests outside East Asia. According to the NDPG, 'the region spreading from the Middle East to East Asia is critical to Japan', thereby mapping Japan's own security interests onto those of the US in the 'arc of instability'. Japan would engage actively in 'international peace cooperation' activities through the dispatch of the JSDF to support US-led and UN multinational operations.[2]

For Japan to fulfill these regional and global responsibilities, the NDPG and MTDP both argue that the JSDF should seek to establish 'multi-functional, flexible and effective' forces characterised by mobility and rapid-reaction capabilities, enhanced joint command and control and the capacity to undertake joint tri-service operations, increased interoperability with UN and US forces, and state-of-the-art intelligence and military technologies. In terms of specific organisation and hardware, the MTDP stresses a quantitative reduction in Japan's Cold War-style forces, and a switch instead to a smaller but qualitatively strengthened JSDF equipped with greater power-projection capabilities.

The 2004 NDPG thus set the agenda for the augmentation of Japanese military power and capabilities over a five-year period that stretched beyond the end of Koizumi's premiership. In early 2009, Japanese security planners were engaged in preparing a revised NDPG for release at the end of the year. The Ministry of Defense started internal discussions on the revised NDPG in 2008 and, as with the revision process of the 1995 NDPO and 2004 NDPG, a new Prime Minister's Advisory Group on Defense was established in Aso's office in January 2009. The Advisory Group is chaired by Tsunehiko Katsumata, the president of the Tokyo Electric Power Company, and consists of senior academics and former government officials.

It is charged with providing an expert and independent report on reformulating the NDPG by mid 2009, to help inform the Ministry of Defense's own efforts. Hence, Japan is engaged in long-term planning for its security policy, and it is within this context that the extent of its remilitarisation should be judged.

Defence expenditure

Assessing Japan's remilitarisation, measured in terms of the size of the defence budget and the number of JSDF personnel, requires a careful methodology and can only partially reveal the extent of military change. Nevertheless, the Japanese defence budget demands examination, first, because any significant change would be a classic symptom of remilitarisation, and second, because Japan itself has long made significant international play of its limited defence budget as a symbol of its restrained military stance.

Measured in US dollar terms (see Appendix: Table 1), the total Japanese defence budget rose strongly between the end of the Cold War and the mid 2000s, reaching between $40bn and $45bn, making Japan the world's third-highest defence spender after the US and France in the late 1990s, and the fourth-highest in 2005 after the US, France and the UK, albeit with the prospect of slipping behind China. These figures are inflated, though, by the relative strength of the yen against the US dollar. If Japan's defence budget is calculated in yen (Table 1), then it has stagnated and actually fallen since the late 1990s, with around $40bn or ¥5 trillion accepted as a de facto ceiling on expenditure. Japan's defence budget in dollar or local-currency terms has not experienced the large-scale growth seen in the US, major NATO states, Russia and even China in the post-11 September period, staying at less than 1% annual growth until 2002, and then contracting to rates of growth between 0.1% and 1.0% until 2008 (Table 1). Defence expenditure is declining in relative importance as a government priority in comparison to the increasing proportion of expenditure devoted to social security and public works in the last decade, declining from around 6.5% of total government spending in the mid 1980s to under 6% by 2008.[3] The amounts available within this tightening defence budget for the procurement of new weapons systems are also under severe pressure. The breakdown of the defence budget demonstrates a long-term trend in which an increasing proportion of funds, 44% by 2008, are directed towards personnel and provisions, with a declining proportion going towards equipment acquisition – from approximately 23% of the budget in 1988 to around 17% in 2008.[4] Japan's defence allocations are under constant pressure from other sectors. Since 2004, the Ministry of Finance has consistently trimmed requests for 1.2–1.5% increases in the defence budget down to below 1%; for 2009, a 2.2% requested increase was cut to 0.8%.[5]

Japan's stagnating defence budget suggests continuing constraints on its remilitarisation. This impression is reinforced by the maintenance of the 1% of GNP limit on expenditure. Prime Minister Takeo Miki first introduced the principle in 1976 to limit criticism of the NDPO.[6] Prime Minister Yasuhiro Nakasone in effect breached the principle by pushing defence spending just above 1% in 1987, although successive administrations have since kept expenditure just below this ceiling (Table 1). Japan's reluctance to increase its defence budget has been a source of frustration not only for the Ministry of Defense and the JSDF but also for the US: US Ambassador Thomas Schieffer called publicly in May 2008 for Japan to increase its defence expenditure to take account of rising defence budgets elsewhere in East Asia.[7] However, while it is clear that the size of the defence budget is an important constraint on Japan's remilitarisation, it also should be noted that Japan has used sleight of hand to maintain the 1% limit, that defence expenditure is thus growing in certain ways and that, in consequence, apparent *quantitative* restrictions have not been an absolute bar on the *qualitative* expansion of Japan's military power.

Japan's defence budget – in contrast to the practice of NATO states with which it always chooses to compare itself in terms of the limits on its defence expenditure in its annual *Defense of Japan* White Papers – excludes military pensions and the costs of the paramilitary JCG.[8] The government has sought to obfuscate the military status of the JCG, with Article 25 of the JCG Law stating that the entity should not be seen as a military unit.[9] Article 80 indicates clearly, though, that the JCG can be regarded as a paramilitary force, due to the fact that, at times of JSDF mobilisation, the JCG can be brought directly under the command of the Minister of Defense.[10] Moreover, as will be seen in Chapter 4, the MSDF and JCG have operated as an integrated force in anti-piracy missions from March 2009. The JCG possesses increasing lethal force for meeting the external maritime threat from North Korea and China, and its budget has expanded during the current decae even as the rest of the defence budget has stagnated.[11] If Japan's defence budget is thus recalculated on a NATO basis, including pensions and the JCG (the figures obtained for the first time here in either Japanese or English), or so-called *kakushi yosan* (hidden budgets), defence expenditure has actually consistently exceeded the 1% of GNP limit since the 1980s, oscillating between 1.1% and 1.5% (Table 1).[12]

Japan has also maintained the pretence of keeping defence expenditure within 1% of GNP, while still managing to find the budgetary flexibility to procure expensive and qualitatively improved military equipment, through the practice of deferred payments (*saimu futan koi*).[13] This has been used since the 1970s to spread the costs of weapon systems over a number of years, building up large-scale future payments equivalent to 60%-plus of defence expenditure (see Appendix: Table 2).

These payments will have to be serviced at some point from the defence budget, and thus may limit the potential for future budgetary growth, but the practice has allowed for considerable flexibility with regard to surpassing the formal 1% limit, and has enabled Japan to continue expanding its military capabilities.

The size and capabilities of the JSDF

Measuring Japan's remilitarisation in terms of the overall size and recruitment trends of the JSDF produces a similarly mixed picture. In line with the 1995 NDPO and 2004 NDPG, the JSDF's overall personnel strength certainly declined since the end of the Cold War. With the disappearance of the threat of a Soviet land invasion, the GSDF in particular has contracted, losing close to a fifth of its regular personnel since the first NDPO in 1976 (see Appendix: Table 3). Equipment levels have also declined, with the GSDF losing almost a third of its main battle tanks (MBT), and the MSDF and ASDF approximately one-tenth of their destroyers and combat aircraft. At the same time, however, the JCG's total tonnage has climbed from 97,000 in 1988 to 126,000 in 2007 (see Appendix: Table 4), and its personnel have increased to around 12,000.[14] A better guide to Japan's military direction in the post-Cold War period, however, is not the quantitative reduction in the size of the JSDF, but rather the qualitative improvement in its military capabilities. As noted at the start of this chapter, the NDPG and MTDP of 2004 sought to convert the JSDF into a 'multi-functional, flexible' force. This has meant the progressive erosion of Japan's opposition to the possession of power-projection capabilities, opening the way for an expanded external Japanese military role in support of US-led coalitions and UNPKO.

The GSDF is seeking to convert itself into a mobile force for overseas operations. It has introduced the 50-tonne M-90

MBT, but is also developing the lighter, 44-tonne TK-X MBT, which is easier to transport, is designed for counter-insurgency operations and has armour that is particularly effective against rocket-propelled grenades and improvised explosive devices (IED) – both weapons commonly used by guerillas. The GSDF also maintains an interest in acquiring 300km-range shore-to-shore missiles for the defence of offshore islands, having originally been denied them in the 2004 NDPG.[15]

The GSDF was dealt a setback in 2009 with the decision to halt procurement of the AH-64D *Apache Longbow* attack helicopter. Japan had procured its first ten AH-64Ds from Boeing, and had planned for Fuji Heavy Industries (FHI) to produce a further 52 under licence. However, the Ministry of Defense was forced to curtail orders due to the rising unit costs associated with licenced production, and instead may opt for upgrading its existing AH-1 *Cobra* attack helicopters or developing an attack version of its OH-1.[16] However, the GSDF's continuing power-projection ambitions were demonstrated by the provision within the 2009 defence budget of additional ballistic protection for its CH-47JA transport helicopters. Japan appears to be following the example of states such as the UK, which has added armour to its *Chinook* helicopters to cope with conditions in Afghanistan and Iraq, suggesting that it is preparing for possible deployment to such theatres if necessary.

The GSDF established a Central Readiness Group (CRG) in 2007, combining the elite 1st Airborne Brigade, 1st Helicopter Brigade, 101st Nuclear, Biological and Chemical (NBC) Unit and the Special Operations Group (SOG). The CRG represents a new departure for Japan. It is intended as a rapid-reaction force for coordinating nationwide mobile operations, responding to domestic terrorism, guerrilla incursions and NBC warfare, and training personnel for overseas deployment. The earlier establishment of the SOG in 2004 reflected a new interest in special forces. Its balaclava-clad personnel paraded publicly during the ceremony marking the establishment of the CRG in 2007. Concealing the identity of military personnel was virtually unheard of in post-war Japan.

ASDF power-projection capabilities have been strengthened through the procurement of the F-2 fighter-bomber (although in smaller numbers than originally hoped for) and the acquisition of an in-flight refuelling capability with the procurement of four KC-767 tanker aircraft (the first was delivered in February 2008). The ASDF is also upgrading its E-767 AWACS aircraft to improve their capacity to detect incoming cruise missiles. Although Japan's signature of the Oslo Convention on Cluster Munitions in December 2008 means that it will dismantle at considerable cost the large stocks of these weapons intended for the defence of its long coastline, the move also offers an opportunity to strengthen the ASDF's capabilities in other ways. For the first time, the ASDF's budget allocation includes fitting its F-2s with joint direct attack munitions (JDAM), providing an arguably more sophisticated defensive, and even offensive, capability than cluster munitions.[17] The ASDF's procurement of JDAM as compensation for the loss of cluster bombs, its continuing interest in airborne electronic warfare equipment and its in-flight refuelling assets should now provide it with the potential to strike against enemy missile bases.

In addition, the ASDF is looking to replace its ageing F-4J fighter-bomber with a new F-X air-superiority fighter capable of besting China's Su-27, J-10 and JF-17.[18] Japan has shown great interest in the US FA-22A *Raptor*, as well as in the Eurofighter *Typhoon* marketed by BAE Systems. The F-22, though, has thus far been denied to Japan by an embargo on overseas sales imposed by the US Congress. During a visit to Washington in April 2007, Abe asked the US to release data on the F-22, and Minister of Defense Fumio Kyuma again raised the issue with

Defense Secretary Robert Gates in a meeting in Washington at the end of the month. The US Congress, however, maintained the ban on exports in July 2008, partly for fear that Japan might leak sensitive technical information given a scandal over failures to maintain safeguards protecting *Aegis* system specifications, and possibly also because of concerns about the impact on the regional balance of power of providing the F-22 to Japan. US Deputy Assistant Secretary of Defense for East Asia David Sedney said in May 2008 that the US was highly unlikely to transfer information on the F-22 to Japan, and that Tokyo should look instead to the F-35 as a new fighter acquisition. Schieffer, the US ambassador to Japan, reiterated this stance in Tokyo the same month.[19]

In the absence of any immediate opportunity to acquire the F-22, and because of the related need to assess other possible candidates for its new fighter, Japan has decided to defer a decision on F-X procurement until the new MTDP for 2010–14. In the meantime, as a stopgap measure the ASDF is investing in upgrades to the radar and AAM-5 air-to-air missiles of its F-15s, to improve their capabilities against both aircraft and cruise missiles. The Ministry of Defense has allocated ¥8.5bn for the Technical Research and Development Institute (TRDI) and Mitsubishi Heavy Industries to conduct research into an Advanced Technology Demonstration-X (ATD-X) stealth-fighter prototype, with an appearance strikingly similar to the F-22.[20]

Japan still seems to harbour hopes that the F-22 might yet be released by the US under the Obama administration. The Ministry of Defense and the ASDF consider the F-22 to be an aircraft that would trump China's capabilities and offer strong interoperability with the US, and see it as a matter of prestige that Japan should deploy the most advanced aircraft available. Influential groups in the US might support the export of the

F-22 to Japan. The US Air Force (USAF) would view Japan's acquisition of the F-22 as an important means of boosting alliance deterrence power in East Asia (with a number of F-22s deployed in Kadena, Okinawa), making up for the claimed deficit in its own F-22 force. Lockheed Martin, Boeing and other US defence contractors might also see benefits in maintaining production lines and technological investment through the transfer of the F-22 to Japan. In February 2007, the Center for Strategic and International Studies (CSIS) released a bipartisan report by former US government officials Richard Armitage and Joseph Nye (Nye was thought to be a possible nominee as US ambassador to Japan under the Obama administration), calling specifically for the US to release the F-22 to Japan as an important measure to strengthen the alliance.[21]

Japan may also need to think seriously about other replacements for the ASDF's F-4Js, especially as the US moves to curtail F-22 orders and possibly to close the F-22 production line. The F-35 would probably meet most of Japan's air-defence needs, and is a true multinational 'alliance' aircraft, offering high interoperability with the US and other allies participating in the programme. However, Tokyo is less well-disposed towards this option because the F-35 is not yet available and, as a latecomer to the programme, Japan would have little opportunity to benefit from technology transfers. Japan might favour new versions of the F-15 and F-18 because of the possibility of technology transfer, but these aircraft are not seen as leading-edge technologically, and the ASDF is likely to view the F-18 as essentially a naval aircraft without sufficient air-superiority capabilities.[22] Japan might find the Eurofighter *Typhoon* a better choice because of its lower price tag ($160–200 million per F-22, versus approximately $100m per *Eurofighter*), and because it would probably be offered the rights to domestic production.

In deferring its decision on the F-X, Japan may try to hold out for the F-22. Japan's possible future success in procuring the F-22, and the very fact that it seeks such a capable fighter and similar stealth technologies, are important indications of its expanding military ambitions. The F-22 would provide Japan with important air-defence capabilities for its own territory. At the same time, though, the ASDF's deployment of the F-22, combined with new in-flight refuelling capabilities (and consistent with the role the aircraft plays for the USAF), would provide Japan with a potential new capability to penetrate and destroy the air defences of any regional adversary, again indicating new power-projection capabilities.[23]

The ASDF is also seeking to augment its power-projection capabilities with an indigenously produced C-X replacement for its C-1 transport aircraft, providing an increased 6,000km range and broadened fuselage for a 26-tonne payload, which will serve as the principal means of air transport for a GSDF rapid-reaction force to regional contingencies and beyond. However, the Ministry of Defense chose not to request the immediate procurement of the C-X in the 2009 defence budget, deciding instead to divert funds to upgrading its F-15s.[24]

MSDF power-projection capabilities have been enhanced through procurement of three *Osumi*-class transport ships, with flat decks for the landing of transport helicopters and an integral rear dock for the operation of hovercraft capable of landing tanks. The MSDF justifies these ships as necessary for peacekeeping and other 'international operations in support of peace', and two of the three have already been deployed to Timor Leste, Iraq, and Indonesia (as part of the humanitarian response to the Indian Ocean tsunami in 2004).

Most significantly, the MSDF is constructing two new *Hyuga*-class DDH (Destroyer-Helicopter) vessels, each displacing 13,500 tonnes deadweight (and approximately 20,000 tonnes when fully loaded with fuels and weapons) and with a standard complement of four helicopters (three SH-60Js and one MCH-101). The first *Hyuga* was commissioned in March 2009. Despite the Ministry of Defense's designation of these vessels as destroyers, the fact that they are the largest ships launched by the MSDF in the post-war period (equivalent in displacement to Spanish, Italian and British helicopter carriers and light aircraft carriers), combined with their 195-metre end-to-end decks and below-deck hangars, their capacity to carry up to 11 helicopters, and their ability to handle the simultaneous landing and take off of up to three helicopters, indicates that Japan is now reviving its expertise in aircraft-carrier technologies.[25]

The MSDF is also indigenously developing the P-X replacement for its P-3C patrol and surveillance aircraft (although Japan has faced pressure to buy the US Multi-mission Maritime Aircraft), with an expanded 8,000km range suited to patrolling as far as the outer reaches of the South China Sea.[26] Japan's security planners, as detailed in Chapter 6, are also showing interest in the acquisition of *Tomahawk* cruise missiles to strike against enemy missile bases.

Japan's other major procurement project is BMD, the largest budget item for 2004–09. The objective is to roll out the full panoply of BMD systems by 2011. The MSDF has procured an off-the-shelf BMD system with a Standard Missile-3 Block IA (SM-3 BLK IA) from the US, and is seeking to fit BMD capabilities to six *Aegis*-equipped *Kongo*- and *Atago*-class destroyers. The MSDF conducted its first successful interceptor test launch off Hawaii in December 2007. The second test in November 2008 proved less successful – the SM-3 interceptor failed to track the target ballistic missile – but nonetheless the BMD *Aegis* system was deemed to have passed most of the test objectives set for it.[27] Japan and the US in the meantime continue to work on upgrades to the interceptor missile to create the SM-3 Block IIA (SM-3 BLK IIA).

Between 2006 and 2008, the ASDF completed the deployment of four *Patriot* Advanced Capability-3 (PAC-3) terminal-phase interceptor batteries, consisting of 16 fire units at bases around Tokyo (Takeyama, Kanagawa; Narashino, Chiba; Iruma, Saitama; Kasumigaura, Ibaraki).[28] The essential responsibility of these batteries is to defend the capital, and the ASDF conducted drills for deployments in Yoyogi Park and Shinjuku Gyoen National Garden in central Tokyo in September 2007 and January 2008.[29] The ASDF also sought to deploy its PAC-3 units to Akita and Iwate Prefectures in the north of Honshu to assist in the possible interception of North Korea's missile test in April 2009. The ASDF successfully tested the PAC-3 system in New Mexico in September 2008.[30] The Japanese government has since February 2007 introduced the 'J-Alert' system to provide warning of ballistic-missile attacks to the Japanese population.[31] The ASDF has also completed the upgrade of its Base Air Defense Ground Environment (BADGE) command and control system to create the Japan Air Defense Ground Environment (JADGE) as the principal coordinator of Japanese air defence in the event of a missile attack. The JSDF is further upgrading the FPS-3UG (Enhanced Capability) ground-based radar and developing a new FPS-5 ground-based radar for BMD purposes.

The JSDF is also attempting to embark on its own US-style 'force transformation' to enable real-time and enhanced coordination of its military forces. Japan has moved towards the indigenous development of unmanned aerial vehicles (UAVs) for coastal battlefield surveillance, including this item for the first time in the defence budget in 2009. The JSDF has now begun joint tri-service operations, experimenting with force integration for the first time during the humanitarian operation that followed the Indian Ocean tsunami, with GSDF helicopters and trucks operating from the MSDF's *Osumi* amphibious ships.

Japan and the militarisation of space

Japanese policymakers began to ease restrictions on the 1969 principle on the peaceful use of space under the administration of Yasuhiro Nakasone (1983–87), with acceptance of the use of satellites for military-communication purposes.[32] However, moves explicitly to breach the principle only gained momentum in the wake of North Korea's *Taepo-dong*-1 test in 1998. The government, driven by the need to improve autonomous intelligence capabilities, and by military-industrial interests keen to exploit procurement opportunities, introduced 'multi-purpose satellites' (*tamoku-teki eisei*) or 'intelligence-gathering satellites' (*joho shushu eisei*) (IGSs).[33] Japan uses this terminology to conceal the military nature of these satellites, which are under the control of the Cabinet Satellite Intelligence Center (CSICE) within the Cabinet Intelligence Research Office (CRIO), again to help disguise the military nature of these procurements. Between 2003 and 2007 Japan launched four indigenously produced IGSs, two optical and two with synthetic-aperture radar (SAR). These satellites have already proved of some use in monitoring North Korea's missile bases, although at resolutions of 1 metre for the optical satellites and 1–3 metres for the SAR they lack the capabilities of satellites deployed by the US.[34] Japan remains dependent on the US for crucial infrared satellite surveillance to detect missile launches, and the early warning necessary to operate any BMD system.

Japan's deployment of spy satellites and BMD has progressively pushed it to breach entirely the anti-militaristic principle on the peaceful use of space. Successive governments have incrementally shifted from the original 1969 interpretation of 'peaceful' (*heiwa no mokuteki*) as meaning 'non-military' (*higunji*) to emphasising instead the 'defensive' military use of space. In June 2007, the LDP introduced a new Basic Law for Space Activities, Article 2 of which states that Japan will conduct activities in space in accordance with the principles of the constitution, thereby permitting the use of space for 'defensive' purposes.[35] The DPJ supported the bill, but its progress through the National Diet was held up in late 2007 by general political deadlock. However, the LDP and DPJ eventually pushed the bill through, and the law was enacted in May 2008.

The Basic Law mandated the August 2008 establishment of a Strategic Headquarters for the Development of Outer Space (SHDOS) within the cabinet, under the direction of the prime minister.[36] The headquarters consists of a number of working groups tasked with researching the strategic, legal and technical aspects of space activities. These are composed of experts on space law, international politics and technology, some of whom are also members of the prime minister's Advisory Panel on Defense.[37] In turn, the Ministry of Defense established its own Committee on the Promotion of Outer Space in September 2008 to advise on space-related activities in the forthcoming revisions of the NDPG and MTDP.[38]

The SHDOS produced a draft report in November 2008 arguing that Japan might need to introduce infrared early-warning satellites for detecting ballistic missiles in their launch phase.[39] The Ministry of Defense Committee on the Promotion of Outer Space produced its first report on 15 January 2009. This argued that Japan should promote the use of communications, global positioning and weather satellites; investigate means to protect its satellites from attack; improve its IGS capabilities; and investigate the acquisition of infrared early-warning satellites to improve the effectiveness of BMD.[40] The LDP Policy Research Council (PRC)'s National Defense Division produced its own report in August 2008, which called for Japan to augment its early-warning systems for BMD by 2015.[41]

Japan's participation in the militarisation of space is clearly driven by its assessment of the regional security environment. Japanese policymakers believe that they must try to catch up with China's burgeoning military space capabilities, and maintain parity with South Korea's and India's military interests in space. Japan further requires enhanced capabilities to keep in step and improve interoperability with the US, and to lessen its dependence on the US for key early-warning satellites for BMD. Japan's ability to develop a full range of satellite capabilities will be constrained by its defence budget, but it seems that the revised NDPG for 2009 and the 2010–14 MTDP will emphasise continuing efforts in this area.

The Japan Coast Guard

The JCG, Japan's maritime paramilitary force, has been quietly augmenting its own capabilities and external power-projection capabilities. The JCG's *Shikishima*-class patrol large helicopter (PLH) vessel displaces approximately 6,500 tonnes and is larger than the MSDF's *Kongo*-class *Aegis* destroyers; it also carries two helicopters, and is armed with two twin 35-millimetre cannons and an M61 20mm gatling gun. It regularly undertakes missions up to 37,000km, having been built to escort plutonium supplies from Europe. The JCG has another 55 vessels displacing more than 1,000 tonnes, many of which are similar in displacement to the MSDF's *Hatsuyuki*-class destroyers. The JCG is reported to have a tonnage close to 60% that of the Chinese People's Liberation Army Navy (PLAN).[42] The JCG also has its own quasi-special forces in the shape of a Special Security Team (SST) for boarding ships, and has long-range early-warning and patrol craft. The JCG has participated in US-led Proliferation Security Initiative (PSI) multinational exercises, and joint bilateral anti-piracy exercises with states in Southeast Asia.[43]

Conclusion

Japanese policymakers argue that the acquisition of the capabilities outlined above does not breach the ban on the possession of power-projection capacity; after all, the MSDF's DDH vessels, even if regarded as light carriers rather than destroyers, are not 'offensive' systems, and the ASDF's in-flight refuelling capability, JDAM and fighters might only be put to use for tactically defensive rather than strategic-bombing purposes. Nevertheless, even allowing for the need to challenge these definitional obfuscations, it is clear at the very least that Japan has now acquired power-projection capabilities for deployment outside Japan. In part, Japan's power projection will be used to provide support for UN peacekeeping activities, but in larger part, and as demonstrated by Japanese 'out of area' deployments, JSDF capabilities provide a new mobile shield for US offensive power in regional and global contingencies. Japan's naval, amphibious and airlift capacities have already demonstrated in US-led coalitions in the Indian Ocean and Iraq some of their future potential for the support of US global power, and these capabilities will be reinforced by the JSDF's helicopter carriers and its sea-mobile interoperable BMD. Moreover, even while current constitutional interpretations and doctrines limit Japan's procurement and utilisation of military capabilities for essentially defensive power projection, many of these capabilities retain latent offensive power, if constitutional interpretations and doctrines shift in the future.

Japan's strategic environment has dictated that it continues to pursue the long-term modernisation of its military forces. The country has had to make difficult choices about new procurement in the context of a constrained defence budget, in some cases delaying or rolling over purchases, and, like any developed state, its ambitions are not always matched by readily available resources. Nevertheless, Japan has succeeded in significantly pushing forward its defensive and potentially offensive power-projection capabilities since the 2004 NDPG. The country is creating a more mobile ground force, an air force with greater regional and global reach and a maritime force with amphibious and carrier technologies. It is moving steadily forward with the deployment of BMD and new space technologies, and the JCG is expanding its capabilities and the range of its missions. Tokyo is in many cases engaged in something of a quiet arms race with China: matching growing Chinese air power with its own enhanced air-defensive power; countering growing Chinese blue-water naval ambitions with its own more capable anti-submarine and carrier assets; and attempting to nullify Chinese ballistic and cruise missiles. Japan's procurement programmes are simultaneously designed to provide the types of capabilities necessary for participation in US-led coalitions.

Japan's ongoing military modernisation has thus not been halted by budgetary constraints or by political tribulations, and is set to continue beyond 2009. The country's evolving regional and global military cooperation with the US, the UN and other international actors continues to push the JSDF towards enhanced power projection. Members of the Prime Minister's Advisory Group on Defense have argued consistently in the past for a more assertive Japanese stance on national defence and for greater US–Japan alliance cooperation.[44] The Advisory Group is thus likely to counsel a redoubling of efforts in these areas, pressing ahead with the F-X, C-X and BMD programmes, and continuing efforts to counter China's rise.

CHAPTER THREE

The Transformation of Civilian Control

Just as important for the remilitarisation process as the size and capabilities of the military establishment is the degree of control over the military exercised by the civilian authorities. Japanese governments in the post-war period have exerted control over the JSDF by concentrating on its professionalisation and separation from politics, while at the same time imposing a high degree of direct civilian management (*bunmin tosei*). According to some analysts, Japan's civilian-control practices have been strict to the point of impeding the basic functions of the JSDF to defend the nation.[1] However, Japan is now seeking to transform civilian-control procedures in an attempt to increase political oversight, expand the influence of the JSDF in security policymaking and enhance its operational flexibility.

Structures of civilian control

Japan's constitution stipulates that all state ministers must be civilians, and the laws establishing the Ministry of Defense, its predecessor the Japan Defense Agency (JDA) and the JSDF state that the civilian prime minister is the commander-in-chief of the JSDF, and directs the civilian head of the Ministry of

Defense, who then gives orders to the uniformed chiefs of the three services of the JSDF. The prime minister is expected to act on behalf of the cabinet, and in consultation with the Security Council of Japan. In addition, the prime minister must obtain *ex post facto* approval from the National Diet for the mobilisation of the JSDF. The prominence of constitutional issues in shaping Japanese security policy has meant that the Cabinet Legislation Bureau (*Naikaku Hoseikyoku*), staffed by elite bureaucrats from a variety of ministries, has played a key role in interpreting Article 9 and its restrictions on the exercise of force.[2]

The framework of civilian control over the JSDF has been buttressed by bureaucratic dominance over the military. The Ministry of Foreign Affairs (MOFA) has taken overall responsibility for devising security policy. In part it has been able to maintain this position through representation on the Security Consultative Committee (SCC), the principal coordinating mechanism for the US–Japan alliance since the Cold War. By way of contrast, the JDA, as the predecessor of the Ministry of Defense, was regarded as a junior partner in security policymaking. For the first half-decade of its life, the JDA lacked full ministerial status and was incorporated into the Prime Minister's Office; many of its top administrative positions were 'colonised' by officials from other ministries, including MOFA, the Ministry of Finance and the Ministry of Economy, Trade and Industry (METI). The JDA's administrative vice-minister and top bureaucrat was generally a MOFA or METI official on secondment.

The JDA exerted similar bureaucratic-civilian dominance (*bunkan tosei*) over the JSDF. The Internal Bureau (*naikyoku*) of the JDA, overseen by defence counsellors (*sanjikan*), advised the defence minister, drafted legislation for the Prime Minister's Office and cabinet, and drafted the director general's instructions to the JSDF's Joint Staff Council (JSC). In effect, this meant that the JSC had only an advisory role in relation to the internal civilian bureaus, rather than being directly consulted by other ministries and the civilian leadership, as is the case in many other developed states. This often resulted in tensions between JDA civilian bureaucrats (*sebirogumi*) and JSDF uniformed officers (*seifukugumi*). The JSDF felt that it was sidelined in decisions about military operations, and that 'civilian control', in the absence of a strong interest in defence issues from elected politicians and the National Diet in the past, had defaulted to unelected 'amateur' officials.[3] Indeed, any sign that the JSDF was seeking to free itself of civilian oversight and attempting directly to devise national security policy was politically explosive, as with the *Mitsuya Kenkyu* incident of 1965, and remarks in 1978 by the chair of the JSC, General Hiromi Kurisu, that, in the event of a national emergency, 'extra-legal' steps might need to be taken to mobilise the JSDF.[4]

Changes in the structure of civilian control

In the post-Cold War period, Japan's structures of civilian control have changed significantly. MOFA has faced progressively stronger challenges to its leadership of security policymaking from the JDA and then the Ministry of Defense. In 1996, the SCC was reconstituted to include the Minister of Foreign Affairs and the director general of the JDA, along with the US Secretary of State and Secretary of Defense. In this '2+2 formula', the JDA achieved parity with MOFA in negotiating with the US. Meanwhile, in January 2007 the JDA achieved its long-sought-for promotion to full ministerial status.[5] The Ministry of Defense's new-found confidence in its status was demonstrated when, in 2007, Takemasa Moriya, a career ministry official and then-administrative vice-minister, resisted attempts to impose a National Police Agency (NPA) secondment as his successor, insisting instead on an internal promotion.

The JSDF for its part has also gained in confidence, and has started to engage in a contest with the JDA/Ministry of Defense to erode bureaucratic control. In 1997, Prime Minister Ryutaro Hashimoto rescinded the 1952 National Safety Agency order, thus enabling JSDF officers to offer direct advice to the Prime Minister's Office and the cabinet.[6] The JSDF is also known to have held consultations with the governing LDP; in one notable case, a serving JSDF officer drafted a proposal to change the status of the JSDF to a 'Self-Defense Military' (*Jieigun*), a proposal which found its way into the LDP's draft plan on constitutional revision.[7] The JSDF officer's association with the LDP was criticised as a possible violation of Article 61 of the JSDF Law, which prohibits serving JSDF members from performing any functions in a political party.

The JSDF has also challenged the defense-counsellor system, resulting in subtle changes in civilian control. The JDA's *Defense of Japan* White Paper in 2003 deleted wording from previous years stating that the civilian administrative vice-minister and defense counsellors assist in the creation of basic defence policy. Instead, only references to the continued role of the political appointees of the senior vice-minister and the two parliamentary secretaries were retained. Successive JDA and Ministry of Defense White Papers have continued with this form of words, although the Establishment Laws of the JDA and the Ministry of Defense have retained articles that stress the role of the *sanjikan* in determining policy.[8] The JSDF pushed for this change in the White Paper in order to diminish the influence of middle-ranking officials, and to open up a more direct route for JSDF officers to provide advice on security policy to the JDA director general.[9] The JSDF stepped up its pressure on the *sanjikan* system with proposals by Chief of Staff Admiral Koichi Furusho at an internal JDA meeting in June 2004. Furusho argued that the planned new JSDF Joint

Staff Office (JSO) should be given equal status with the civilian administrative vice-minister and defense counsellors, and direct access to the senior vice-minister and the two parliamentary secretaries.[10] Furusho later publicly argued that the chief of staff of the JSO should not be subject to the control of the JDA's civilian bureaucrats.[11] The LDP's Defense Policy Studies Subcommittee proposed in March 2004 that the defense-counsellor system should be reviewed, and Shigeru Ishiba, the then-director general of the JDA, ordered an internal review of the system from August 2004 onwards.[12] The JSDF was not entirely successful in overturning the defense-counsellor system, as the review concluded that it should be retained and that civilian officials should still serve as the buffer between the director general and the JSDF.[13]

However, the JSDF has continued to strengthen its own policy cohesion and presence within the defence structure through the creation of the JSO in March 2006, designed to facilitate joint operations between the three services. The previous decision-making structure for joint operations among the three elements of the JSDF consisted of the JSC and the three chiefs of staff of the GSDF, MSDF and ASDF. This had hampered joint operations as the JSC functioned more in an advisory than command role in executing the JDA director general's policy, and each chief of staff was able individually to provide advice to the civilian leadership, the result in practice being that each service acted separately in accordance with its own doctrine.[14] The new JSO, with its chief of staff drawn from the GSDF, the MSDF or the ASDF, now represents all three services, and has become the principal military conduit for relaying civilian orders to the JSDF. It is also potentially capable of acting as the principal military adviser to the Minister of Defense.[15]

Japan's civilian-control structure has further changed due to the new operational demands resulting from the introduction of

BMD, and the need for an extremely rapid response in the event of a ballistic-missile launch. In February 2005, legislation was passed to amend the JDA Establishment Law. This new legislation, carried over into the Ministry of Defense Establishment Law, now enables the Minister of Defense to mobilise the JSDF to launch interceptor missiles with the approval of the prime minister, rather than in consultation with the Security Council of Japan, as mandated under the previous law. In situations where there is no time to consult the prime minister, the Minister of Defense is entitled to order the JSDF to launch interceptors in accordance with pre-planned scenarios.[16] This gives greater freedom to JSDF commanders in the field than would have been imaginable in the decades following the end of the Second World War.

Civilian-control regimes have thus eroded, as the JDA and Ministry of Defense have gained in confidence and the command structures of the JSDF have become increasingly integrated. Although it might be argued that this growth in the military establishment's influence constitutes a 'normalisation' of the role of the military bureaucracy and officer elites, the process may have served neither to maintain effective civilian control nor to improve military operability.

Civilian control: failures and reforms

It has become apparent that the JSDF and the Ministry of Defense have failed to report accurately to the top civilian leadership concerning the MSDF's refuelling activities in support of US-led coalition naval vessels operating as part of *Operation Enduring Freedom*. The MSDF correctly reported to its own Chief of Staff Office in February 2003 that it had supplied the US with 800,000 gallons of fuel oil, but this information was wrongly recorded as 200,000 gallons and then passed on to the director general of the JDA and the chief cabinet secretary. At the same time, the JDA/Ministry of Defense's Internal Bureau was provided with the correct information, but chose not to correct the figures or inform senior levels within the JDA/Ministry of Defense that they were inaccurate.[17] The fact that these mistakes went unreported for more than four years has been interpreted in Japan as a fundamental failure of civilian control, made even more worrying by the fact that it involves overseas Japanese forces operating close to a conflict zone and far from the oversight of the political leadership. Consequently, the Cabinet Secretariat in December 2007 established a Ministry of Defense Reform Council (*Boeisho Kaikaku Kaigi*) to consider ways of improving civilian control, defence-information security and defence procurement. The Ministry of Defense launched its own internal Reform Promotion Team in February 2008 to investigate measures to ensure civilian control.[18]

The future shape of civilian control resulting from these reform efforts is beginning to emerge. Ishiba, reappointed to the defence portfolio in September 2007, argued in both committees in February 2008 for a radical overhaul of civilian-control measures within the Ministry of Defense. His plan advocated the abolition of the strict hierarchy of civilian control over uniformed officers, and argued instead that bureaucrats and officers should work equally alongside each other in new integrated bureaus, in a system modelled on that of the UK.[19] Ishiba's intention was to increase information-sharing between bureaucrats and officers in order to improve military efficiency and provide greater support for the ministerial appointees tasked with exercising civilian control.[20] Ishiba's plan faced resistance, though, from bureaucrats concerned at losing control over the military and personnel numbers within the Ministry of Defense, and to some extent from JSDF officers concerned at the possible diminution of the cultures of the individual services.

Elements of the Ministry of Defense's revised plans were announced in April 2008 and involved the creation of a new internal Defense Council (*Boei Kaigi*), designed to be the supreme decision-making body in the ministry for discussing general defence policy and the operation of the JSDF in contingencies.[21] The plan, again involving a degree of integration of civilian bureaucrats and uniformed officers, entails the abolition of the *sanjikan* system, and the institution of new ministerial defence advisers drawn from among retired JSDF personnel and the private sector, thus once again elevating the status of the JSDF in the policymaking process. Meanwhile, the LDP's PRC Subcommittee on Ministry of Defense Reform put forward similar but more radical plans in April 2008, proposing to abolish the Internal Bureau's Operational Policy Bureau and fully integrate civilian bureaucrats and uniformed officers in the Internal Bureau and the JSO, and arguing that the JSO's chief of staff should be able not only to relay orders to the three heads of the GSDF, MSDF and ASDF, but actually operate JSDF units directly. In addition, the LDP proposed providing the prime minister with special advisers drawn from the JSDF and Ministry of Defense.[22]

The Ministry of Defense Reform Council released its final report in July 2008. This argued that the principal concern in reforming civilian-control procedures was not the fear that Japan's military could once again ignore civilian democratic procedures, but that the effectiveness of Japan's military operations should be improved.[23] To this end, the report confirmed the recommendation that the prime minister's command functions over the Ministry of Defense and JSDF should be strengthened through closer meetings with the chief cabinet secretary, the Minister for Foreign Affairs and Minister of Defense; the establishment of a ministerial meeting on the build-up of defence capabilities; and the inclusion in the Prime Minister's Office of military and civilian experts as aides. It was recommended that the Ministry of Defense establish a Defense Council and abolish the *sanjikan* system and the Internal Bureau's Operational Policy Bureau; transfer the execution of JSDF operations to uniformed JSO officers by assigning a civilian bureaucrat of up to deputy-director level in the JSO; restructure the Internal Bureau's Defense Policy Bureau by adding to its staff a JSDF officer as deputy director; and integrate the procurement functions of the Internal Bureau and the three JSDF services.[24] The report thus argued for stronger roles in defence policymaking for Japan's political leaders, for the JSDF, and for the two in cooperation, with a concomitant reduction in civilian bureaucrats' influence. For some Japanese policymakers, especially Ishiba, the report apparently did not go far enough in integrating non-uniformed and uniformed officials, causing some disagreement with then-Prime Minister Fukuda.[25] Nonetheless, the report became the basis for the Ministry of Defense's initiation in July 2008 of a Ministry of Defense Reform Head Office, to follow up on and implement the recommended reforms.[26] Its basic report, released in December 2008, essentially confirmed that the Cabinet Secretariat's recommendations would be followed.[27]

The Tamogami affair

The debate on transforming civilian control was reignited in October 2008 by an incident involving the ASDF's Chief of General Staff, General Toshio Tamogami. The APA Group – a hotel chain headed by Toshio Motoya, a known historical revisionist, associate of former Prime Minister Abe and key supporter of a local association with links to the ASDF's Komatsu base in Ishikawa Prefecture – announced on 31 October that Tamogami had been awarded the top prize of ¥3m (about $30,000) in its essay competition. Tamogami, who had come to know Motoya from his time as commander of Air Wing 6 at Komatsu, had entered the competition, entitled 'The True Outlook for Modern and Contemporary History', in May 2008 with an essay called *Was Japan an Aggressor Nation? (Nihon wa Shinryaku Kokka de Atta no Ka?)*. The competition was judged by Shoichi Watanabe, a professor at Sophia University, another revisionist and a denier of the Nanjing massacre.

Tamogami made a number of highly controversial claims in the essay, including that Japan advanced into the Korean Peninsula and mainland China during the colonial period on the basis of international treaties, was inadvertently drawn into the Second Sino-Japanese War of 1937, brought the benefits of liberation and development to Korea, Taiwan and Manchuria, liberated East Asia from Western colonialism from 1941 onwards and was ensnared by the US into launching the attack on Pearl Harbor. Tamogami criticised the International Military Tribunals for the Far East for placing the entire blame for the war on Japan, thus creating a type of 'mind control' among the Japanese people and casting them as aggressors. Tamogami argued that, as a result, in the post-war period the JSDF had been overly restricted in prosecuting its mission to ensure national security, in terms of the ban on the exercise of collective self-defence and on possessing offensive weapons.[28]

In the wake of the award's announcement, the government removed Tamogami from his post. Tamogami's expressed views directly contravened the government's official positions on responsibility for colonial aggression and the exercise of collective self-defence.[29] Japanese policymakers were also concerned over the damage that might be caused to US–Japan relations, and to relations with China and Korea (both of which quickly condemned Tamogami's stance). Minister of Defense Yasukazu Hamada removed Tamogami from his position as

ASDF chief of staff on 31 October, and the Ministry of Defense announced his retirement on 3 November.

The Tamogami affair nonetheless rumbled on, not least because Tamogami himself refused to demonstrate any contrition. In a press conference following the announcement of his retirement, Tamogami claimed that his essay was historically correct, and argued that attempts to muzzle his criticisms of official government policy were akin to the restrictions on free speech in North Korea.[30] In addition, by 7 November it had become clear that Tamogami had encouraged a number of other ASDF officers, later found to total 97, the majority from the Komatsu base and Air Staff Office, to submit essays to the same APA Group competition. (Motoya later confirmed that they contained similar revisionist views.[31]) Further revelations soon emerged that, during his stint as head of the Joint Staff College from 2002 to 2004, Tamogami had established lecture courses on Japan's wartime past which included speakers with strongly revisionist views and connections with the controversial Japanese Society for Textbook Reform (*Atarashii Kyokasho o Tsukurukai*).[32] Tamogami, it seems, also submitted a revisionist essay to the May 2007 issue of *Hoyu*, an internal ASDF journal, but escaped sanction by the Ministry of Defense.[33]

Tamogami's apparent challenge to his civilian superiors was compounded by the fact that he had defied explicit requests from Prime Minister Aso to resign.[34] In the end, the Ministry of Defense was obliged to demote Tamogami and allow him to retire with full benefits, including a ¥60m retirement bonus. Thereafter, Tamogami caused a further rumpus when he was summoned by the DPJ to present evidence to the National Diet on 11 November, in hopes of embarrassing the government in the midst of debates on the passage of the RSSML. Tamogami made a confident appearance, again asserting the historical accuracy of his views and his right to free speech; Japan, he said, should revise Article 9 of the constitution to allow collective self-defence; public opinion supported his stance, and if necessary he would summon 'a thousand' ASDF officers to write similarly revisionist pieces.[35] Aso afterwards sought to play down the affair, stating in the National Diet on 13 November that, while Tamogami's views were inappropriate for a member of the JSDF, it certainly would be a 'leap too far to suggest that this represented some form of coup d'etat' (*'sore ga tadachi ni kudeta ni naru toka to iu no wa shosho, hanashi ga hiyaku shisugi'*).[36]

Arguably, the Tamogami affair manifested the growing confidence of the JSDF and its opposition to the traditional post-war strictures of civilian control.[37] Tamogami's resistance to civilian direction was reminiscent for some of the behaviour of the pre-war Japanese military, and was even described as a 'verbal coup' against the constitution and civilian control.[38] The fact that Tamogami was able to climb to the top of the JSDF structure holding such views, and was allowed free rein to propagate them within the ASDF, demonstrates an important failure of civilian control.

It also demonstrates that the Ministry of Defense Reform Council was perhaps premature in stating that Japan's military would never again ignore democratic and civilian procedures. The council considered the Tamogami affair at a meeting in December 2008 primarily intended to discuss the Ministry of Defense Reform Head Office's basic report released the same month. The council stressed the need for more balanced historical education for the JSDF, but also noted that, to prevent similar incidents in the future, it was important to press ahead with its recommended reforms, especially the increasing integration of uniformed officers, bureaucrats and political leaders to promote correct debate among them on history issues.[39]

Conclusion

Japan's civilian-control structures are facing a serious challenge from a Ministry of Defense and JSDF gaining in confidence and desiring enhanced freedoms in order to respond to the perceived exigencies of national security. Japan's traditional structure of bureaucratic-civilian control has been eroded by pressure from the JSDF, and the reform efforts of the Ministry of Defense have been directed towards increasing political, as opposed to bureaucratic, control. The Tamogami affair and public concerns over civilian control appear not to have deflected Japanese policymakers from pushing for enhanced integration and greater contact between politicians, the military and bureaucrats. The influence over defence policymaking enjoyed by Japan's military thus continues to increase.

These changes may improve the JSDF's operational flexibility, and the system may function well as long as political leaders are competent to oversee it. However, the fact that the Ministry of Defense has suffered repeated changes of leadership since attaining full ministerial status in 2007 (Fumio Kyuma, September 2006–July 2007; Yuriko Koike, July–August 2007; Masahiko Komura, August–September 2007; Shigeru Ishiba, September 2007–August 2008; Yoshimasa Hayashi, August 2008–September 2008; Yasukazu Hamada, September 2008 to date), and that Japan as a whole has had three prime ministers in that time, does not augur well for the necessary political continuity to offset declining bureaucratic oversight.

CHAPTER FOUR

Japan's Military-Industrial Complex

Japan's defence production and the question of the rise of a military-industrial complex demand investigation because, as pointed out in the Introduction, these have often been presented as key barometers of remilitarisation. In particular, the Japanese government has been able to argue in the post-war period that it has not fallen foul of the types of military and industrial linkages which drove procurement in the pre-war period, and that it has been able to maintain a restrained military stance due to the limited nature of defence-industrial collaboration with the US, and the 1967 and 1976 prohibitions on arms exports.[1] Hence, any change in the internal structure of defence production, and in external linkages regarding transfers of military technology and weapons, are key indicators of long-term remilitarisation.

Japan's domestic military-industrial complex

Japan cannot be said to have possessed anything akin to a fully fledged military-industrial complex in the post-war period. In its initial stages, the US-led Occupation, alongside its broader demilitarisation and democratisation reforms, emphasised the dissolution of the *zaibatsu* (industrial conglomerates), which were viewed as having colluded with the ultranationalists and the military in pushing ahead with Japanese imperialism in the interests of their own defence-production profits. The dissolution of the *zaibatsu* as an element of demilitarisation was allowed to wane, however, following the outbreak of the Korean War and the lifting by the Occupation authorities of the defence-production ban in 1952. Thereafter, Japan began to rebuild its defence-production sector through its own rearmament and through procurement contracts from the US military.

In preparing for the end of the Occupation, Japan's policy-makers never lost sight of the importance of maintaining an indigenous defence-production base to strengthen national autonomy and bolster the overall economy. Nevertheless, Japan's post-war defence planners, even as they attempted to pursue wherever possible the building up of indigenous defence-production capabilities (*kokusanka*), rejected a policy of massive defence spending and the promotion of large-scale defence contractors. Instead, Japan, in line with domestic constraints on defence spending, would sustain its military-technological base by re-embedding it within larger civilian and industrial conglomerates.[2] Japan's domestic defence production was subordinated to civilian developmental priorities, with the civilian sector drawing technological 'spin-off' from the military sector, and where necessary the smaller military sector deriving 'spin-on' technology from its civilian counterpart.[3]

Consequently, Japan's defence-production sector has been small relative to the overall national economy, accounting since the 1980s for less than 1% of total industrial production.[4] A similar picture emerges in relation to most key industrial sectors, although military shipbuilding accounts for between 5% and 10% of total Japanese shipbuilding, and military aircraft for between 60% and 80% of national aircraft production.[5] Japanese defence production has been concentrated within a relatively small number of conglomerates focused predominantly on civilian production. Mitsubishi Heavy Industries (MHI) has remained the leading Japanese defence contractor in terms of sales and contracts. Other main players include Kawasaki Heavy Industries (KHI), FHI, Toshiba, Ishikawajima Harima Heavy Industries (IHI), Mitsubishi Electric Company (MELCO), NEC and Komatsu. Trading companies such as Itochu and Sumitomo are involved in importing defence equipment. These companies dominate Japanese defence procurement, with over 70% of total contracts, but defence tends to account for a relatively small proportion of their overall business.[6] MHI, despite taking nearly a fifth of total defence contracts, derives less than 10% of its total sales from this sector; for others the share is smaller still, at less than 4%.[7] Japanese corporations globally rank low in terms of total defence sales and the percentage of their business derived from defence.

However, even if Japan does not have the classic features of a military-industrial complex, there has been collusion in the past between the JDA, the JSDF and defence contractors. This has taken the form of *amakudari* (literally 'descent from heaven'), or the placing of retired bureaucrats and uniformed officers on the boards of companies; the role of the LDP's *boei zoku* (literally 'defence tribe'), consisting of policymakers seeking to influence if not broader policy on weapons acquisition, then at least the patronage to be dispensed to their constituencies through defence contracts; and a high degree of discretionary (non-competitive bidding) contract awards, typically around 80% of the total value of all contracts.[8]

These practices appear to have intensified in recent years. For instance, the former director general and deputy director general of the JDA's Central Procurement Office were arrested in September 1998 for allowing defence contractors to pad out procurement contracts, obliging the JDA to abolish the office in January 2001 and split the functions of contracting and costing in an attempt to assure more rigorous checks on equipment procurement. In another scandal in January 2006, officials from the Defense Facilities Administration Agency (DFAA) were arrested for colluding with private construction and electronics firms in the award of defence contracts. The DFAA was dissolved and its functions absorbed into the Ministry of Defense in September 2007.

The Ministry of Defense became embroiled in its most significant procurement scandal to date in October 2007, involving former Administrative Vice-Minister Moriya. Moriya was convicted in November 2008 of receiving around ¥12m in hospitality and cash bribes from Motonobu Miyazaki, a former employee of the Yamada Corporation and president of the Nihon Mirise Corporation, in order to influence procurement decisions in favour of Miyazaki. Moriya admitted using his influence within the Ministry of Defense to steer it towards signing discretionary contracts with Nihon Mirise for the supply of General Electric (GE) engines for C-X aircraft and 19DD destroyers. Moriya also received bribes from an Itochu subsidiary to secure a discretionary contract for the import of two *Eurocopter* helicopters for the GSDF.[9] The scandal also threatened to involve former defence ministers Fukushiro Nukuga and Fumio Kyuma, who were known to have associated with Miyazaki.[10]

The Moriya scandal exposed for the first time the extent of the links between politicians, bureaucrats and elements of the defence industry, and the government is concerned that it represents deepening structural corruption. The Ministry of Defense Reform Council revealed in 2008 that, over the previous five years, around 500 retired JSDF personnel had requested permission under the JSDF Law to take up positions with commercial enterprises, including almost 200 former officers of colonel or naval captain rank and above, and that the most popular destination for these personnel were companies involved in Ministry of Defense procurement; the most popular new employers were MHI, NEC and MELCO.[11] In 2006, the JDA revealed to the National Diet that, in 2004, 718 retired JSDF personnel were working in firms with JDA contracts, again mostly concentrated in MHI affiliates.[12] The JDA/Ministry of Defense is also believed to associate with defence contractors through the exclusive social grouping of the '*Hinoki-kai*', comprising executives of section-chief level and above.[13]

The Ministry of Defense has attempted to curb this emerging military-industrial complex through a series of internal ministerial and wider government reform panels dealing with the Central Procurement Office, DFAA and Moriya cases. In response to the Moriya scandal, the Ministry of Defense Reform Council and the ministry are seeking ways to increase transparency in procurement procedures, and monitoring more carefully the pricing practices of the trading companies handling overseas procurements.[14] However, as all the reform panels have concluded over the last decade, Japan faces a problem of essentially structural corruption due to the relatively young retirement age and delayed pensions, by international standards, of Ministry of Defense bureaucrats and JSDF officers, and contractors seeking to offer re-employment in return for information on defence procurement.[15]

Japan's defence-production sector is arguably beginning to exhibit the features of a military-industrial complex. The defence sector displays signs of deep structural collusion between the bureaucracy, politicians, industry and the military. It is hard to assess how novel this is, given the difficulties, for instance, of obtaining statistics for the *amakudari*.[16] The repercussions of the scandals touched on here may also have been magnified by enhanced media scrutiny. However, what appears to be strikingly new about Japan's emergent domestic military-industrial complex – and thus what has most perplexed the government in the wake of the Moriya scandal – is the concern that collusion has escalated to the extent that interest groups are not only, as in the past, extracting patronage from defence contracts, but are threatening to take control of overall defence-procurement policy and direct it without reference to broader national-security interests.

Japan's emerging transnational military-industrial complex

For much of the post-war period, Japan has been to a significant degree divorced from international military production. Japan's emphasis on maintaining indigenous production has been one factor making for a degree of autonomy and autarky in the defence sector (with domestic procurement levels accounting for almost 90% of total expenditure).[17] The other factor, of course, has been Japan's self-imposed ban on the export of weapons technology.

Japan was a significant exporter of weapons-related items to the US military engaged in the war effort in Vietnam and to allied militaries in Southeast Asia until the imposition of the 1967 and 1976 bans, and since then has continued to maintain significant foreign military sales (FMS) procurements from the US. It has also licenced production of key US weapons systems and has embarked on 13 co-development projects with Washington since the 1980s, the most notable of which was the FS-X/F-2.[18] Japan has exported dual-use technologies with military applications to China, Southeast Asia and Africa, but it can state with conviction that, since the 1960s, it has not engaged in significant arms transfers to spur militarisation in other regions.[19]

Since the late 1990s, however, Japan has been forced to reconsider its defence-production policy and expand international linkages. The defence industry is beset by the twin problems of limited demand in Japan itself, due to tight defence budgets, and lack of access to co-development partners and economies of scale for increasingly expensive weapons systems, as a result of the ban on arms transfers. There has been some consolidation in Japan's defence industry, especially in military shipbuilding (IHI and Sumitomo Heavy Industries moved their military-shipbuilding activities into IHI Marine United in 1995; in September 2001 IHI, KHI and Mitsui Zosen formed a workshare agreement; in October 2002 NKK and Hitachi integrated their military shipbuilding into Universal Shipbuilding; and in October 2002 KHI formed Kawasaki Zosen, a new subsidiary shipbuilding company).[20] But Japan by and large has found consolidation difficult due to its post-war model of embedding production capabilities within larger civilian conglomerates, which can thus not easily be separated without damaging civilian production. A number of firms are quitting the defence industry altogether.[21] The Japanese government has sought to maintain an indigenous defence-production base by initiating new projects, such as the P-X and C-X aircraft, and there are plans for a stealth-fighter prototype, all designed to nurture 'strategic' and 'specialist' technologies and to preserve the potential for systems integration and building larger platforms. But despite these efforts, and a plethora of government and industrial advisory reports, the JDA concluded in 2005 that Japan's defence-production base was 'seriously weakening'.[22]

Japan now has little choice but to consider increasing international collaboration, and its policymakers and industrialists have fixed upon a partial or total lifting of the arms-export ban.[23] In January 2004, in his first stint at the JDA, Ishiba gave a speech at The Hague touching on the need to lift the ban on exports to facilitate joint defence production with the US and other countries. The Prime Minister's Office later stressed that the government was considering this solely in relation to the US and BMD. Nevertheless, Ishiba's remarks reflect strengthening opinion within the JDA/Ministry of Defense and segments of domestic industry regarding the need to end the export bans. The LDP's Defense Policy Studies Subcommittee in 2004 proposed that the total ban be lifted in favour of an export-licencing scheme.[24] This call was repeated by the Defense Production Committee of the *Keidanren*, Japan's leading business association, in July 2004.[25] Also in 2004, Abe, at the time the LDP's secretary-general, advocated a return to the principles of the 1967 ban on arms exports to communist countries, countries under UN sanctions and states party to conflict, thereby clearing the way for high-tech weapons sales and co-production with other developed states.[26] The Prime Minister's Council on Security and Defense Capabilities, in preparing for the revision of the NDPG in 2004, commented that expanding technological military cooperation with states other than the US should not be seen as Japan acting as a 'merchant of death'.[27] Hopes for a wholesale revision of the arms-export ban were eventually dashed by the intervention of the LDP's dovish coalition partner, New Komeito.[28] However, the ban was partially lifted in December 2004 in order to facilitate the co-development of BMD with the US, although the chief cabinet secretary's statement stressed that this did not conflict with the ban because the project was designed to promote the smooth functioning of the US–Japan alliance and enhance Japan's own defence.[29]

The Japanese defence industry has inevitably looked to the US as its prime international partner, seeing the advantages of producing highly interoperable equipment for alliance cooperation, and the possibility of accessing leading-edge technologies. For its part, the US favours co-development in order to share costs and gain access to advanced Japanese manufacturing techniques and certain technologies. The main bilateral project is the upgrading of the SM-3 BLK-IIA interceptor missile for the *Aegis* BMD system, which will eventually move into some form of co-production involving the deeper integration of US and Japanese industry, either through the wholesale exchange of technologies or the establishment of a joint plant in Japan or the US. In 2007, the Armitage–Nye report cited above advocated the lifting of all further restrictions on Japanese arms exports to the US.[30]

It is not far-fetched to imagine the eventual emergence of a US–Japan transnational military-industrial complex. The two countries' defence industries have been allied since 1996 through the US–Japan Industry Forum for Security Cooperation (IFSEC), chaired by MHI and Boeing and consisting of the DPC, the Japan Defense Industries Association and leading defence contractors in both countries.[31] The IFSEC has advocated increased defence-production cooperation and the lifting of the arms-export ban.[32]

The Moriya procurement scandal further demonstrated the strength of US–Japan political, military and industrial links when Naoki Akiyama, executive director of the Japan–US Center for Peace and Cultural Exchange (the Center), was convicted in November 2008 of accepting payments from Yamada Corporation to assist in persuading the Ministry of Defense to employ the company as a sales agent for GE C-X engines, and to act as the subcontractor for the disposal of poison-gas shells abandoned by the Imperial Army in Fukuoka Prefecture.[33] Motonobu Miyazaki, the prime figure involved in bribing Moriya, stated in Diet testimony in May 2008 that he had paid Akiyama ¥100m to deal with potential difficulties in disposing of the shells that might arise from 'fishing interests and organised crime' in Fukuoka.[34] Miyazaki had been a member of the board of the Center until 2006, a board packed with prominent political, bureaucratic and industrial figures from both states, including former Japanese Ministers of Defense and a US Secretary of Defense.[35]

The Center is associated with the Congressional National Security Research Group (NSRG) (*Anzen Hosho Giin Kyogikai*, also known in Japanese as *Anzen Hosho Kenkyusho*). Akiyama served as the Office Director, and the NSRG drew on many of the same Japanese Diet members. The Center and NSRG, in conjunction with the Heritage Foundation in the US, has been responsible for organising the Japan–US Security Strategy Conference (*Nichibei Anzenhosho Senryaku Kaigi*), which invites a number of prominent figures to discuss alliance-related issues such as BMD technological cooperation. Meetings usually include speakers from US and Japanese industry, and have featured presentations by Raytheon, Boeing, Lockheed Martin and Northrop Grumman.[36]

The ban on arms exports is also being challenged in other ways. The chief cabinet secretary's statement of 2004 has now been interpreted by the Ministry of Defense as providing grounds for investigations with other countries into joint research and development in response to terrorism and piracy.[37] Japan has exported 'demilitarised' ex-JCG patrol craft to Indonesia for anti-piracy activities, and has embarked on new, if small-scale, international defence-technology cooperation.[38] The TRDI has dispatched observers to Sweden's NBC-warfare research facilities, and has used French facilities for stealth-fighter technologies. Japanese policymakers also see possibilities for international cooperation in technologies to clear landmines and lessen the threat from IEDs, and, as discussed above, have shown interest in the Eurofighter *Typhoon* as a possible replacement for the F-4J. Japan's construction companies may also become involved in a form of external remilitarisation by bidding for contracts to build overseas military facilities for the US. The Japan–US agreement on meeting the costs of relocating US Marine Corps bases from Okinawa to Guam explicitly contains rights for Japanese companies to bid for work constructing these new facilities. Hence, the indications are that, as the problems facing Japan's domestic defence industry grow amid stagnant budgets and rising unit prices for equipment, it will gradually seek to re-enter the international military co-development and export markets.

Conclusion

Collusion between industrial, political, bureaucratic and military elements in Japan's defence-production structures has increased, a sign of significant remilitarisation. Similarly, Japan's emergent transnational military-industrial complex has involved increasing de facto breaches of the anti-militaristic principles banning the exports of armaments, and thus marks a significant turning away from one of the key features of its demilitarised stance in the post-war period. It might be argued that Japan is only doing what is 'normal' for other major states, in terms of the globalisation of military production and the effort to search out export markets, but it cannot be denied that this constitutes a departure from its previous stance on arms transfers, and an escalation in Japan's remilitarisation. The manner in which Japan is remilitarising may also give grounds for concern, with the transnational military-industrial complex driven in part by narrow US–Japan commercial interests, which has generated suspicions of collusion.

CHAPTER FIVE

Japan's External Military Commitments

Japan's external remilitarisation needs to be assessed not just in terms of the direct deployment of its own military forces overseas through the mechanism of the US–Japan alliance and UN-centred activities but also through Japan's expanding physical and financial support of US regional and global power projection, in the form of the provision of bases and the integration of military capabilities. In terms of overseas deployments and the restructuring of the US–Japan alliance in the post-Koizumi period, there has been some retrenchment and progress has been slower than Japanese and US policymakers would have liked. Nonetheless, despite domestic political controversy over the dispatch of forces overseas, Japan has persevered with the restructuring of its alliance with the US and has continued to search for ways to deploy the JSDF abroad. Japan has therefore continued to enhance its overseas military commitments.

JSDF missions in Iraq and the Indian Ocean

Japan has found it difficult to maintain its two most prominent overseas missions in the post-9/11 period: MSDF support for *Operation Enduring Freedom* (OEF) in the Indian Ocean, and

GSDF and ASDF participation in the reconstruction of Iraq. Japan's commitment to these missions marked an important precedent in that it was the first time the JSDF had been sent overseas during ongoing conflicts, albeit in non-combat roles, and the two missions were taken as important symbols of Japan's support for the US and the international community in the fight against transnational terrorism and the proliferation of weapons of mass destruction (WMD), and of its future commitment to expanding international security cooperation.

Since 2006, however, Japan has curtailed its commitments to these missions. The 600 GSDF troops serving in Samawah, Muthanna Province, Iraq, were withdrawn in July 2006 after the completion of their two-year mission, in part because it was thought that their main reconstruction goals had been achieved. According to the Ministry of Defense, the GSDF had provided 53,000 tonnes of water, repaired 36 schools and 66 medical facilities, completed 31 roads and given employment to over 1,000 Iraqis.[1] In large part, though, the GSDF had to be 'redeployed', and relatively quickly, because the planned handover of security in the province to Iraqi forces was brought forward, and the British and Australian forces providing protection for the GSDF were withdrawn. Two years later, in December 2008, the ASDF's five-year operation flying UN and coalition materials and personnel from Kuwait to Baghdad and Erbil in northwest Iraq came to an end. The ASDF is reported to have flown a total of 821 missions, transporting 46,500 personnel and 673 tonnes of cargo.[2] The Japanese government decided to withdraw the ASDF because the UN resolutions mandating coalition missions in Iraq were about to expire, and because the US and other coalition partners were drawing down their own forces. In addition, the government was aware that the DPJ was considering using its new strength in the National Diet to force an end to the mission.

In the end the JSDF's exit from Iraq was made with a certain amount of haste, in response to changing international circumstances and domestic pressures. It is also uncertain whether the JSDF mission was more a hindrance than a help to coalition operations. Japan's resistance to anything other than a non-combat mission (there were only three GSDF (non-fatal) casualties, caused by road accidents in June 2006, and not a single shot was fired in anger in five years of deployment) meant that protection had to be provided by other coalition forces. Moreover, the mission was extremely costly, and made only a questionable contribution to reconstruction. The GSDF's provision of water supplies and contributions to other reconstruction activities were arguably far more expensive than equivalent provision by NGOs or even local employees; medical equipment donated by the GSDF could not be maintained afterwards by Iraqi personnel, not least because the instructions were in Japanese; and the GSDF's rapid withdrawal meant that it could not finish its road-mending work, leaving long stretches unmetalled.[3]

The MSDF's mission in the Indian Ocean has also come under international and domestic pressures and has faced similar criticisms. Since 2001, Japan has sought to maintain one or two destroyers and a fuel-supply ship on station in the Indian Ocean; according to the Ministry of Defense, between December 2001 and October 2007 the MSDF refuelled coalition ships 794 times with a total of 490,000 kilolitres of fuel, and provided helicopter fuel 76 times to a total of 990 kilolitres. The MSDF supplied warships from the US, UK, France, Germany, Pakistan, Canada, New Zealand, the Netherlands, Italy, Spain and Greece.[4]

The DPJ sought to block renewal of the ATSML authorising the deployment in 2007. The DPJ is opposed to the mission because it argues that Japan is in essence providing support to US and coalition missions for the use of force in Afghanistan and possibly other theatres, thus breaching the ban on collective self-defence. The DPJ used the issue to force Abe's resignation in 2007, and then proceeded to oppose Fukuda's attempts to renew the mission. The DPJ was given extra leverage with the revelations in late 2007 that the MSDF had incorrectly reported fuel-supply figures, and there were suspicions that the US had diverted Japanese fuel to operations in Iraq. In a September 2007 report based on unclassified US data, the Japanese NGO Peace Depot suggested that the MSDF had supplied fuel to the US aircraft carrier *Kitty Hawk* in 2003, and that the ship had then immediately engaged in the Iraq War, thus contravening the purpose of the ATSML, which is specifically designed to support *Operation Enduring Freedom* alone.[5] Supported by additional information from the US, the Ministry of Defense denied these accusations.[6]

Fukuda succeeded in passing the RSSML in January 2008, but the DPJ's continuing opposition to renewing the legislation at the end of 2008 contributed to his resignation. His successor, Aso, forced the RSSML through the National Diet again in December 2008. Despite DPJ opposition, therefore, successive administrations have managed to maintain the MSDF mission in the Indian Ocean, though only by incurring mounting domestic political costs, limiting the MSDF to refuelling only and obliging all recipient navies to guarantee that the fuel supplied will only be used as part of *Operation Enduring Freedom*.[7]

The MSDF deployment to the Indian Ocean was Japan's first and most high-profile action in support of the US 'war on terror', and still forms a key symbolic commitment to US and international counter-terrorism efforts. However, the fact that Japan has found it hard to maintain even this moderate commitment, combined with the humiliation of the MSDF's temporary withdrawal from the Indian Ocean in November 2007, necessitated by DPJ opposition to the renewal of the ATSML, and the speedy departure of the GSDF from Iraq, inevitably raises questions about Japan's willingness to undertake overseas missions, and the future of the MSDF deployment in the Indian Ocean remains in doubt.

However, while Japan's problems in Iraq and in the Indian Ocean have set back its international security ambitions, these are in many ways minor and temporary difficulties. Policymakers have generally seen these operations as highly successful, laying the foundations for the long-term, incremental expansion of Japan's overseas commitments. Hence, rather than focusing purely on the specific contribution of the Iraq and Indian Ocean missions themselves to international security, Japan has used them to gain experience of operating in international coalitions. The JSDF has now worked alongside the US and other militaries in the Indian Ocean and Iraq, and has sent personnel to US Central Command (CENTCOM) in Tampa, Florida, to participate in coalition planning.[8] If UN peacekeeping operations are included alongside the Iraq and Indian Ocean missions, it is estimated that, by 2002, there were 3,000 Japanese personnel deployed overseas at any one time. Around 5,500 GSDF personnel served on rotation in Iraq, and by 2007 approximately 30,000 JSDF personnel had gained overseas experience.[9] Japan has expanded the range of weaponry available to the GSDF overseas, starting with pistols in earlier missions and building up to include assault rifles, machine guns, recoilless rifles and light anti-tank ammunition. The JSDF was also given a new mandate to use these weapons to protect its own personnel and others under its responsibility, including refugees and injured US service personnel. Both the Indian Ocean and Iraq missions have provided important precedents for future JSDF deployments outside Japan. Indeed, Japanese security policymakers, despite problems in the renewal of the RSSML, are seeking new missions and coalition partners.

The Indian Ocean tsunami, Afghanistan, the Permanent Dispatch Law and anti-piracy missions

In addition to the missions in Iraq and the Indian Ocean, Japan has explored a variety of new avenues for dispatching the JSDF overseas. Under the International Disaster Relief Law, the JSDF undertook its largest-ever single overseas operation in response to the Indian Ocean tsunami, deploying a total of 1,500 personnel, diverting MSDF ships returning from the Indian Ocean to Japan to deliver relief assistance, and in January 2005 sending a flotilla including an *Osumi*-class transport to Aceh in Sumatra following the tsunami. The flotilla, carrying five GSDF helicopters and 20 trucks, acted as a 'floating camp' for joint MSDF and GSDF operations. Through its participation in the relief operation, the JSDF gained valuable experience in joint and combined operations, and of operating with the US and other states in a multinational environment, through the establishment of a coordinating liaison headquarters alongside the US at the Thai military base of Utapao.[10]

Japanese policymakers have also shown renewed interest in UNPKO as a way of increasing the JSDF's overseas operational experience, though the fact that, in early 2009, just over 30 JSDF personnel were deployed on such operations, out of a total military strength of close to 240,000, demonstrates that Japan's real policy energy remains focused on participation in US-led or UN-authorised coalition-type missions. Twenty-nine GSDF personnel have been deployed as part of the peacekeeping mission to the Golan Heights since 1996; six liaison officers were dispatched to the UN Political Mission in Nepal (UNMIN) in April 2007 for a one-year deployment; and in mid 2008 Japan considered joining the UN Mission in Sudan (UNMIS), in part as a response to China's growing peacekeeping presence in Africa.[11] In the end, two liaison officers were sent to the UNMIS headquarters in Khartoum.

The political problems involved in renewing the legislation associated with the Iraq and Indian Ocean missions have prompted Japanese policymakers to seek more routine means to deploy the JSDF overseas. In August 2006, during his tenure as chief cabinet secretary, Abe raised the possibility of a permanent dispatch law (*kokyu hoan* or *ippanho*) for the JSDF, removing the need for the government to engage in time-consuming debates and pass separate time-bound laws for each mission, thus enabling the JSDF to engage more rapidly in 'international peace cooperation operations'.[12] Abe raised the issue again in January 2007, during an address – the first-ever by a Japanese prime minister – to the North Atlantic Council, raising hopes within NATO of Japanese military assistance in Afghanistan.[13] Minister of Defense Kyuma discussed the mooted law and a JSDF commitment to Afghanistan with NATO officials in May 2007.[14]

As his administration began in September 2007, Fukuda appeared less enthusiastic about a permanent dispatch law, preoccupied as he was with defence-related scandals. However, by early 2008, following the difficulties surrounding passage of the RSSML, he had begun to warm to the idea. Fukuda was also aware of growing demands from the US and NATO for the JSDF to step up its efforts to support *Operation Enduring Freedom* beyond refuelling, and to assist the coalition on the ground in Afghanistan. Finally, Fukuda perhaps saw the permanent dispatch law as a means of forging a compromise with the DPJ over JSDF overseas commitments; in October 2007, DPJ leader Ichiro Ozawa had argued that the JSDF might be sent to Afghanistan, potentially even for combat duties, if it was mandated to do so by appropriate UN resolutions.[15]

In January 2008, Fukuda instructed the LDP's PRC to initiate a Project Team (PT) to study the feasibility of submitting a permanent dispatch law to the National Diet later in the year, based on the principles that JSDF deployments would be within the bounds of the constitution, in accordance with requests from the UN and other international organisations and limited to non-combat zones, and would require approval by the National Diet.[16] Then-Minister of Foreign Affairs Masahiko Komura repeated Japan's intention to pass a permanent dispatch law at the Munich Security Conference in February 2008.[17] Japanese leaders subsequently hinted that they would pass legislation and deploy the GSDF as part of the International Security Assistance Force (ISAF) in Afghanistan, including a statement to this effect by Ishiba at the IISS Asia Security Summit in May. Japan then received direct requests from the US and NATO for the GSDF to provide helicopters and C-130s to make up for shortfalls within the coalition, with the GSDF, as noted in Chapter 2, beginning to armour its CH-47JA helicopters for these type of missions.[18] However, by the latter part of 2008 it had become clear that Fukuda's government was unlikely to press ahead with a permanent dispatch law. The LDP itself, and its New Komeito coalition partner, became concerned at the risks of JSDF entanglement in combat operations in Afghanistan as the security situation appeared to worsen.[19] Japan has aborted plans to send the JSDF to Afghanistan, and has settled instead for increasing its contribution to ISAF through funding upgrading of NATO coalition helicopters, and increasing financial support for Provincial Reconstruction Teams (PRTs).[20] In early 2009, it appeared that the Obama administration in the United States was content with this additional financial contribution as it prepared to step up its own forces in Afghanistan.

Japan's policymakers are now focusing on MSDF anti-piracy activities off the coast of Somalia and the Gulf of Aden. Aso in particular has argued since March 2008 for these types of operations as a means of expanding and redefining US–Japan security cooperation.[21] Japanese interest in anti-piracy activities was stimulated by UN Resolution 1816 in June 2008, which provided a potential mandate for JSDF participation in Combined Task Force (CTF) 150. Interest was heightened by the hijacking of the *Sirius Star* and other high-profile pirate activities towards the end of 2008, drawing attention to Japan's own problems with piracy in the region. In mid October 2008, Aso stated that Japan might consider passing a new anti-piracy law to enable the deployment of the MSDF, a suggestion that drew support from a cross-party grouping of LDP and DPJ politicians.[22] Finally, and decisively, in late December news came that China had decided to dispatch two destroyers to the Gulf of Aden, raising fears in Japan that China might use the opportunity to expand cooperation with the US.[23]

Japanese policymakers have decided on a two-stage approach to deployment in order to ensure conformity with constitutional and legal requirements. The first stage is the stop-gap measure of dispatching the MSDF under the maritime-police-action provisions of the current JSDF Law. These enable the JSDF to provide protection for Japanese shipping or other shipping with Japanese crew or Japan-related cargo. The JSDF would be permitted to use force against pirates in self-defence and to facilitate emergency evacuations, and to order suspected pirate ships to halt and be boarded. JSDF deployments are to be reinforced by the presence of eight JCG personnel on the destroyers, because under the current law the MSDF lacks powers of arrest, whereas the JCG is able to detain and gather evidence for the prosecution of pirates.[24]

Officials in the Ministry of Defense and MSDF charged with carrying out the anti-piracy mission have felt that existing legal provisions are inadequate to ensure effective operations and the safety of Japanese personnel in the event of a confrontation with pirates prepared to use force against them. Hence, the second stage of the response has been the preparation of a new anti-piracy law by an LDP–New Komeito PT.[25] The new legislation should allow the JSDF to protect non-Japanese ships as long as they are in the same vicinity, and to use force not only for self-defence but also to compel pirate vessels to halt if no other reasonable means is available.[26] The government argues that the use of force against pirates to protect foreign shipping does not equate to collective self-defence because it is essentially a police action against a non-state actor.[27] The deployment of the JSDF would be approved by the prime minister and then reported to the National Diet, thereby avoiding the problems experienced in gaining prior sanction for the ATSML/RSSML.[28]

The government planned to submit the new anti-piracy law to the National Diet in March 2009. The fact that the bill was supported by the LDP and New Komeito, and that many DPJ members sympathised with the anti-piracy cause, suggested that it would be passed relatively quickly. However, the bill is controversial in that, despite official arguments to the contrary, the provisions enabling the protection of non-Japanese ships do appear to touch on questions of collective self-defence, and the bill entails a clear loosening of the restrictions on the use of force. The government has sought to assuage these concerns by stipulating that ships under Japanese protection must be close by, thus blurring the distinction between self-defence and collective self-defence.

In January 2009, the Ministry of Defense ordered the destroyers *Sazanami* and *Samidare* to prepare for deployment. The destroyers will carry the MSDF's Special Boarding Unit (SBU). The Ministry of Defense is also looking into sending P-3C patrol aircraft to the CTF 150 headquarters in Djibouti once it has concluded a Status of Forces Agreement (SOFA).[29] In February 2009 the ministry carried out a fact-finding mission around the Gulf of Aden, in Djibouti, Bahrain, Yemen and Oman, in order to prepare for the deployment of the MSDF; the destroyers departed for the Gulf of Aden on 14 March, to begin anti-piracy patrols by early April.

Although this individual commitment is again modest, Japan's participation in anti-piracy efforts will be a useful addition to international security efforts. More importantly, it will enable the JSDF to expand and prolong its presence in the Indian Ocean and beyond. The deployment of destroyers, JCG personnel and P-3Cs, and possibly an additional fuel-supply ship, combined with the existing RSSML deployments, will provide the Japanese military with considerable power-projection capabilities in the region.[30] The fact that an estimated 2,300 merchant ships of concern to Japan pass through the Gulf of Aden region annually will ensure that the MSDF remains on station for the long term.[31] The anti-piracy mission will again provide the MSDF with valuable experience of working alongside the US and other states in a multinational environment; indeed, in February 2009 Japan and South Korea even discussed the possibility of joint patrols.[32] Moreover, the anti-piracy law's new provisions on protecting foreign ships and the use of force may set useful precedents for JSDF missions in the future if Japan again considers passing a permanent deployment law.[33]

Security ties with the US, Australia and India

Japan has also begun to forge security links to complement its alliance with the US. Japan and Australia have been engaged in low-key security cooperation since the 1970s, but stepped up bilateral ties in the late 1990s, and especially in the wake of the 'war on terror' with the deployment of the Australian Defence Force (ADF) to protect the GSDF in Iraq.[34] Japan's intention has been both to strengthen bilateral links with Australia and also to embed them within the wider structure of the US–Japan alliance and US regional security ties. In May 2005 Japan, the US and Australia established an annual Trilateral Security Dialogue (TSD), running in parallel with efforts to upgrade the US–Japan alliance through the DPRI process. Prime Ministers Koizumi and Abe appeared to see the TSD as an important means of mobilising the three key democracies in the region in order to counter China's rise. The two were also keen to forge a 'Strategic and Global Partnership' with India, including cooperation on maritime security, and Abe was receptive to attempts by the Bush administration to develop quadrilateral security cooperation between Japan, the US, Australia and India.[35] The four powers plus Singapore held joint naval exercises in the Bay of Bengal in September 2007.

Four-way cooperation has not advanced as rapidly since 2007 due to Fukuda's caution, lest Japan be seen as trying to contain China. However, bilateral security ties between Japan and Australia have progressed with the signing in March 2007 of a Japan–Australia Joint Declaration on Security Cooperation (JADSC). The JADSC stresses broad cooperation on issues such as WMD proliferation, as well as more direct military cooperation, including in peacekeeping, defence exchanges, search and rescue and participation in the Proliferation Security Initiative (PSI).[36] In June 2007, Japan and Australia established their own '2+2' foreign- and defence-ministers' dialogue to mirror the Japan–US SCC, and concluded a 'Comprehensive Strategic, Security and Economic Partnership' in June the following year. Military cooperation is limited, however, by Japan's constitutional restrictions, and because the ADF is over-stretched in meeting its commitments.[37] Nevertheless, Japan and Australia have scope for building cooperation through sharing intelligence in the Indian Ocean and South China Sea, PSI and anti-piracy activities, and Australia's provision of a satellite ground station at Lansdale, Western Australia, to support Japanese IGS capabilities. Japan and Australia are also bound together through their integration into US global and regional strategy for missile defence, with Australia providing relay ground stations at Pine Gap in the Northern Territory to feed launch-detection data from US satellites to Japan.[38]

Change and realignment in the US–Japan alliance

Japan in the post-Koizumi era has continued its external remilitarisation by exploring a variety of means to extend and expand the overseas deployment of the JSDF. But Japan's external military commitments have been promoted even more significantly in recent years by the continued strengthening of its alliance with the US, which is a major contributor to US global military hegemony. Japanese policymakers, both before and after Koizumi, have become increasingly aware that the US expects its regional allies not only to contribute military forces to multinational coalitions, but just as importantly to provide greater flexibility in allowing the US to use bases for regional and global deployments. In seeking to remain an indispensable ally and to maintain political and strategic leverage over the US, Japan has thus sought, in conjunction with efforts to dispatch the JSDF overseas, to focus on restructuring alliance cooperation within its national territory, in order to facilitate the projection of US power.

The DPRI is the outcome of these efforts. The first stage involved the release by the SCC in February 2005 of agreed common regional and now global objectives for the alliance (see Appendix: Box 1). The following October, the SCC laid out a set of specific areas where bilateral military cooperation would be enhanced, with a particular emphasis on improving interoperability, intelligence exchange and the sharing of base facilities.

In May 2006, the SCC released a 'Roadmap for Realignment Implementation'. This was designed to enhance the capacity of the US–Japan alliance to respond to security crises, while also reducing the burden US bases impose on local communities, particularly in Okinawa, which hosts a disproportionate share of US military facilities in Japan.

Japan's acceptance of the relocation of the US Army's I Corps (a rapid-deployment force with a geographical ambit covering the Asia-Pacific and the Middle East) from the continental US to Camp Zama in Kanagawa, beginning in 2008, implies that Japan will now serve as a frontline command post for US global power projection. Japanese policymakers have long acknowledged that the US has utilised its bases in Japan for deploying forces outside the geographical scope of the security treaty, which is limited to the Far East. This was shown in the dispatch of US Marine Corps and Seventh Fleet assets from Japan to fight in the Iraq War. Japan has, however, maintained that these forces must first be deployed from Japan to an area in the Far East and then redeployed to the Middle East, meaning that they are not direct deployments under Article 6 of the treaty. In line with the DPRI, policymakers have now reconciled themselves to a de facto breach of previous interpretations of the geographical scope of the treaty as covering only the Far East and Asia-Pacific, a change they have justified on the grounds that US deployments outside the region may contribute to Japan's security, and are permissible as long as they do not hamper US ability to defend Japan.[39] Japan's relocation of its CRG rapid-reaction force to Camp Zama between 2008 and 2012 will further strengthen interoperability in power projection between the US and Japan.

Alliance cooperation between Japan and the US also continues in BMD. Japan's agreement under the DPRI to establish a Bilateral Joint Operations Coordination Center (BJOCC) at

Yokota, co-locating ASDF and US air-defence systems, will increasingly entail the sharing of sensor information and the integration of Japanese and US BMD forces. The SCC confirmed in May 2007 that the US and Japan were committed to the 'routine sharing of BMD and related operational information directly with each other on a real-time, continuous basis'.[40] Under the DPRI, Japan has also permitted the US to deploy additional BMD assets, including an X-band radar system at Kashiri in Aomori Prefecture, PAC-3 in Okinawa and, since 2006, BMD-capable *Aegis* destroyers, further strengthening bilateral cooperation in this area. Cooperation has also been reinforced by joint drills since 2005 to exchange BMD sensor information, Japanese tests of SM-3 missiles off Hawaii in 2007 and 2008, and by the joint project to upgrade the BMD interceptor missile. Japan and the US were also coordinating closely in the run-up to North Korea's scheduled missile test in April 2009, with Japan mobilising two of its *Aegis* BMD destroyers and the US deploying five missile-defence-capable *Aegis* cruisers around Japanese territory.[41]

Japan's closer cooperation with the US, and possession of an *Aegis* BMD system largely interoperable with that of the US, is likely to increase US expectations that Japan will deploy these assets in support of US and multinational coalitions outside its territory, possibly in combat situations. There are also expectations that Japan's BMD system should function if necessary for the defence not just of Japan but also of the US homeland. US policymakers and officials, including Ambassador Schieffer, Deputy Under-Secretary of Defense for Asia-Pacific Affairs Richard Lawless and Secretary of Defense Robert Gates, have progressively made it clearer that the US expects Japan to use its BMD assets to help intercept missiles targeted at their country.[42] In addition, the SCC in May 2007 agreed that both countries would 'clarify concepts, roles, and missions for each side in the conduct of missile defense and related operations in response to ballistic missile threats', a statement interpreted by the Japanese media as requiring Japan to investigate the use of BMD assets to assist in the defence of the US itself.[43] Thus, even though Japan has resisted overtly integrating its BMD system into US global plans for missile defence, it has implicitly become a key and inextricable component in the support of US regional and global power in this area.

Japanese and US attempts to extend the boundaries of alliance cooperation in recent years have not been without difficulties. The DPRI negotiations proved arduous and took longer than expected. The US frequently became frustrated with Japan's apparent fixation on domestic politics, seeking to reduce the basing burden on local communities rather than concentrating more closely on alliance interoperability. Hence, US policymakers labelled the DPRI more of a 'real-estate' bargain over bases than a negotiation among allies with genuine new strategic objectives in a post-11 September world.[44] The US was further frustrated by Japan's reluctance, once the DPRI was concluded, to discuss a fresh revision of the Guidelines for Defense Cooperation. Japan has thus continued to try to limit where possible its alliance commitments to the US; in particular, it has continued to obfuscate its stance on military support in the event of another crisis over Taiwan.

Koizumi's successors have also found it hard to implement all the measures agreed in the 2006 Roadmap at a pace satisfactory to the US. In May 2007, Abe's government passed a Law to Promote the Realignment of US Forces in Japan, providing for necessary finance and local-government subsidies to underwrite the relocation of US bases to Guam. Japan and the US then entered into protracted negotiations, with Japan keen to ensure that its original estimated contribution of $6bn to the total $10bn relocation costs did not increase, and that there was sufficient transparency to ensure that Japanese financing was used only for building the new Marine Corps facilities on Guam. These negotiations have not been helped by opposition from the DPJ, which is concerned at the overall cost and transparency. Most frustrating for both Japan and the US, there is still no sign of substantial progress on the key issue of relocating the USMC Air Station from Futenma to Nago. Okinawa Prefecture is requesting a change to the location of the new runway at Nago on safety and environmental grounds, and the Japanese government has yet to decide whether it is amenable to this change, while the US insists that the location, agreed under the DPRI, should stand. Both sides have been searching for a solution to the Futenma issue for over a decade. Japanese policymakers have some grounds for optimism regarding the DPRI, though, as Iwakuni City eventually agreed in March 2008 to accept the relocation of the US carrier wing from Atsugi. Hence, the pieces of the complex DPRI jigsaw are incrementally falling into place.

There have also been differences at a wider strategic level. Japan has been concerned that the US has not sufficiently reciprocated recent changes in the alliance by increasing its support for Japan's strategic interests and great-power ambitions. Japanese policymakers were dissatisfied with the Bush administration's merely passive support for their bid for a permanent UN Security Council seat in 2005, were disgruntled by the administration's refusal to provide the F-22, and were dismayed by the US's effective abandonment of Japan over the issue of Japanese abductees in North Korea, in pursuit of a nuclear deal with Pyongyang at the end of 2008. The Bush administration for its part was at times unsettled by Japan's confrontational stance towards China under Koizumi and Abe over historical questions, and towards North Korea over its nuclear programme and the abduction issue, to the point of hindering progress in the Six-Party Talks. US officials were also irritated by public criticism of their occupation policy in Iraq by Kyuma and Minister of Foreign Affairs Aso. (Aso called the US occupation 'naïve', and Kyuma's unflattering remarks led the US to reject a Japanese proposal for a defence summit.[45]) Security ties have also been troubled by difficulties with host-nation support (HNS) financial provision for US bases. The DPJ and opposition parties blocked a new HNS agreement in the National Diet in March 2008 citing a lack of transparency, forcing the Japanese government to ask the US to meet basing costs in the interim before it could use its super-majority to push the HNS budget through the following May. Finally, security ties have been periodically affected by criminal incidents involving US personnel in Okinawa and on mainland Japan.

Despite these difficulties and disagreements, Japan and the US have largely continued to forge ahead with the long-term strengthening of the alliance. Joint exercises have been stepped up, with around 30 held annually. For the first time, in February 2007, the GSDF and the US Marine Corps held joint exercises on the US mainland at Camp Pendleton, California, simulating the retaking of Japanese territory. Japan for the first time accepted the home-porting of a US nuclear-powered aircraft carrier, with the deployment of the USS *George Washington* to Yokosuka in September 2008 to replace the soon-to-be-retired conventionally powered *Kitty Hawk*. The Japanese public has expressed concerns about nuclear safety, but Tokyo's determination to press ahead with the deployment of the *George Washington* represents an important element in the strengthening of US naval power around Japan and in the Asia-Pacific, given the carrier's higher speed, extended range and larger on-board fuel supplies for its aircraft. Japan and the US also concluded a General Security of Military Information

Agreement (GSMIA) in August 2007, designed to bolster the exchange of military information in the wake of scandals associated with the leak of *Aegis* system data, and to bring Japan in line with most major US allies.[46] Japan was even reported in November 2008 to have begun work with the US on new planning for regional contingencies, with Tokyo finally beginning to designate specific civilian air and seaports and medical facilities for the US to use in a conflict.[47] Japan and the US thus may have achieved a deeper level of war-planning than at any time in the post-war period.

Military cooperation between the US and Japan looks set to increase under the Obama administration. During a visit to Japan by Secretary of State Hillary Clinton in February 2009, the two sides finally signed an agreement on the relocation costs of Marine Corps units to Guam, which was to be submitted to the National Diet for approval in March 2009. Indeed, the Obama administration may take a slightly different tack on alliance cooperation, possibly shown by its relatively relaxed attitude to the possibility that the JSDF might not be deployed to Afghanistan. In contrast to the Bush administration, Obama's team may be less concerned with the physical deployment of Japanese troops and sailors, and may instead seek a greater Japanese contribution in terms of finance and JSDF defensive capabilities in and around Japan itself, so as to allow the US to project power more freely in East Asia and globally.

Conclusion

In the post-Koizumi period, the Japanese government has undoubtedly found it harder to maintain external military commitments, as shown by the difficulties it has faced over renewing the MSDF mission in the Indian Ocean and by the withdrawal of the GSDF and ASDF from Iraq. However, Japan has worked to maintain its foothold in the Indian Ocean, and has quietly explored a range of ways to enable the deployment of the JSDF to Afghanistan and in anti-piracy missions. Japan is also feeling its way towards new military ties with Australia and India. Meanwhile, alliance cooperation with the US continues to deepen through the DPRI process. Progress might have slowed since the Koizumi administration, but many of the key elements involved in the restructuring of alliance cooperation have been followed through, including enhanced interoperability between the JSDF and the US military, the acceptance of new, more capable US military assets on Japanese soil for regional and global power projection, greater flexibility under the security treaty for these assets to be deployed outside Japan, and support for US global missile-defence systems.

The US alliance has long been viewed by the US, China and other regional states as a means to suppress the resurgence of Japanese military power – as then US Marine Corps commander Lieutenant-General Henry Stackpole famously put it in 1990, acting as the 'cap in the bottle' of Japanese militarism. Nevertheless, the US itself has progressively encouraged the expansion of Japan's external military role within the framework of the alliance.

CHAPTER SIX

The Erosion of Japan's Anti-militaristic Principles

Japan's remilitarisation can be seen not just in changes in its material military capabilities and alliance relationships but just as significantly in the erosion of the deep-seated institutional and societal attitudes which have constrained its military posture in the post-war period. These changes are manifest in Japanese public attitudes towards the status of the country's military forces; the weakening of the taboo on the acquisition of nuclear weapons; moves towards revision of Article 9 of the constitution; the introduction of more 'patriotic' or nationalist education; greater public acceptance of certain forms of security activities; and, finally, an acceptance of the use of force for national-security ends.

The JSDF's societal status

The JSDF, in contrast to the armed forces of many other developed states, has occupied a lowly position in Japanese society in the post-war period. It has striven to dissociate itself from the pre-war Imperial Japanese Army and Navy's domination of society, and has sought to blend into civilian society as much as possible. It is striking that, in a society in which everyone from schoolchildren to taxi drivers to department-store workers wear uniforms, JSDF personnel rarely wear uniforms off-base for fear of social derision.[1] JSDF personnel, either in uniform or who are known to be in the military, have been assaulted by members of the public, and have been called 'tax thieves' by those who believe the existence of the military is an unnecessary use of national resources.

In the past, the JSDF has found it difficult to recruit personnel. Cabinet Office opinion surveys reveal that, for much of the post-war period until the early 1990s, public approval and disapproval of a career in the JSDF were finely-balanced (see Appendix: Chart 1). The main reasons for approval were the JSDF's role in defending Japan, the honour of the profession and the group lifestyle it embodied (Chart 2); disapproval was based mainly upon the physical dangers of military service, an outright rejection of the necessity of the JSDF itself, the availability of other employment and simple ignorance of the JSDF as a profession (Chart 3). For most of the post-war period, if seen as useful for anything in the public's eyes, the JSDF was accorded a past and future role often primarily in domestic natural-disaster relief operations (Charts 4, 5 and 6). Ensuring national security was sometimes a secondary function.

Since the early to mid 1990s, however, the JSDF's societal reputation has considerably improved, while the reasons for public support have changed. The JSDF's image overall has steadily improved, reaching record positive ratings of around 55% by 2006 (Chart 7). The JSDF's most useful role is still seen as providing domestic disaster relief, a view bolstered by the Hanshin-Awaji earthquake in 1995 (Charts 5 and 6).[2] At the same time, however, the Japanese public are increasingly supportive of the JSDF's role in defending national security, to the point that this now rivals domestic disaster relief as its perceived primary function (Charts 4 and 6). The JSDF's rising profile in public security, including responding to spy-ship incursions from North Korea, seems to be linked to new fears about the penetration of Japan by North Korean guerrilla forces. The JSDF's new roles in UN peacekeeping and in 'international peace cooperation activities' have further boosted public support (Charts 5 and 6). The JSDF also appears to be regarded as a more legitimate actor in defending Japan against foreign aggression. Although the Japanese public itself seems no more willing than in previous years to take up arms to resist invasion directly, its willingness to support the JSDF actively in doing so appears to have increased (Chart 7). The JSDF, overall, has managed to promote a far more acceptable public face as a safe and essential presence in Japanese society. Indeed, the Japanese military has even become fashionable through its 'manga-isation' in publicity and recruitment materials, which use popular cartoon and animation stylisation to communicate a safe and comforting image.[3] In turn, Japanese public approval for the JSDF as a profession has outstripped disapproval ratings since the mid 1990s. This approval is based on increasing acceptance that the military serves to preserve Japan's national security; that it possesses a new role in international security cooperation; and that it is now a more legitimate organisation (Chart 2). Disapproval ratings still derive from perceptions of the dangers of military service in wartime and the harshness of military life in general. However, it is noticeable that disapproval based on low levels of social esteem have declined, as has the proportion of Japanese people who do not accept the JSDF as legitimate (Chart 3).

Hence, even as the JSDF has contracted in overall size in the post-Cold War period, this rise in the societal status of the military as a career seems to have enabled the overall successful recruitment of the authorised number of volunteer personnel. JSDF recruitment levels have picked up since the mid 1990s, moving from around 88% to 96% of authorised numbers, with a particularly significant improvement in GSDF numbers, the staffing rate of which has climbed from 84% in 1995 to just over 90% in 2008 (Table 5). (Maintaining the quality of personnel, however, is always a concern for the Ministry of Defense: in 2008, for instance, the ASDF admitted that it would have to lower the standards for pilot recruits' eyesight, as the number of suitable applicants had fallen by over half since 2005, and from 2009 onwards female personnel will be allowed to serve on destroyers, minesweeper tenders and the *Hyuga* helicopter carriers, to alleviate some crucial personnel shortages.[4]) Although this boost in recruitment is to some extent accounted for by Japan's prolonged recession in the 1990s, during which the JSDF served as an employment refuge, opinion polls are clear that approval of the military as a profession has grown since the early 1990s, based on the perception that it provides training in useful skills applicable to other future careers, and that military pay and conditions have improved (Chart 2). In part, the boost in numbers – despite Japan's shrinking population and contracting pool of candidates for recruitment – also represents a genuine increase in the popularity of the JSDF as a worthy calling in the defence of national security.[5]

Eroding anti-nuclearism?

Japan's nuclear-weapons stance has long been debated and any change closely watched for as a decisive turning-point in its remilitarisation.[6] The nuclear debate was stimulated most recently by North Korea's nuclear test in October 2006, which raised questions about Japan's continued adherence to the Three Non-Nuclear Principles of 1967 (not to produce, possess or introduce nuclear weapons).

In reaction to the North's test, Shoichi Nakagawa, then-chairman of the LDP's PRC, initiated a debate on the potential utility of Japan acquiring its own nuclear deterrent. Nakagawa stated on a popular TV Asahi talk-show programme on 15 October that 'there exists a logical argument that the possession of nuclear weapons lowers the probability of being attacked, and thus it would be appropriate to debate this'.[7] On 18, 19 and 25 October, then-Minister of Foreign Affairs Taro Aso weighed in with remarks in the National Diet to the effect that, while the government had no intention of breaching the Three Non-Nuclear Principles, it was important that nuclear armament was freely debated.[8] Nakagawa repeated his calls for a debate during a visit to the US on 27 October, and again in Japan on 30 October and 5 November, although he stressed that he was speaking in a personal capacity and was not necessarily advocating the acquisition of nuclear weapons.[9] In a speech in Hamamatsu, Shizuoka Prefecture, on 20 October, Nakagawa also reportedly suggested that North Korean leader Kim Jong Il could launch a nuclear attack against Japan because of possible irrationality caused by his diabetes.[10]

On 15 October, Abe responded to Nakagawa's initial remarks by stressing Japan's intention to preserve the Three Non-Nuclear Principles, and saying that debate on the issue was finished.[11] However, Abe then demonstrated some ambivalence during questions in the National Diet on 8 November by indicating that members of his government and party, even while holding to the stance of not debating Japan's official non-nuclear stance, would inevitably discuss issues of future nuclear deterrence in the wake of North Korea's nuclear test.[12] Abe only fully shut down discussion on Japan's nuclear option with a statement on 21 November at the Asia-Pacific Economic Cooperation (APEC) summit that the LDP and the government would not debate possessing nuclear weapons.[13]

This flurry of domestic comment attracted considerable international attention as the US and neighbouring states began to speculate about Japan's nuclear intentions and the ramifications for regional security. On 16 October, President Bush noted his concern that Japan's possible reconsideration of its nuclear stance would cause anxieties for China, and that North Korea's possession of nuclear weapons might produce a nuclear arms race in Northeast Asia.[14] Then-Secretary of State Condoleezza Rice voiced similar concerns, although she also expressed her confidence that Japan would not seek to acquire nuclear weapons.[15] At the same time, a number of conservative US commentators raised the possibility of encouraging Japan to acquire nuclear weapons in order to assist in deterring North Korea and to intimidate China into exerting pressure on Pyongyang over its nuclear programme.[16] Meanwhile, both China and South Korea stressed the need for Japan to preserve its non-nuclear stance.[17] South Korea's then-foreign minister and UN secretary-general-elect, Ban Ki-moon, during a news conference at the Japan National Press Club in Tokyo on 6 November, voiced his concerns over Japanese politicians' discussions about the possibility of developing nuclear weapons in response to North Korea.[18]

Attempts to stimulate a debate on nuclear weapons, and the international attention it received, are not unsurprising given the gradually intensifying discussion of Japan's nuclear stance in the post-war period. Japan has maintained a nuclear option since Prime Minister Nobusuke Kishi's statement in the National Diet in 1958 that the country was constitutionally entitled to possess nuclear weapons if it deemed them necessary for the country's defence.[19] Despite receiving the Nobel Peace Prize in 1974 for introducing the Three Non-Nuclear Principles (these were, in fact, largely a device to nullify opposition from the left on security and to assist in freeing Okinawa of US nuclear weapons upon its reversion to Japanese administration in 1972), Eisaku Sato was the most pro-nuclear of Japanese leaders, reportedly privately describing the principles as 'nonsense'.[20] Sato himself breached the principles by allowing the introduction or transit through Japanese ports of nuclear weapons on US vessels, and following China's successful nuclear tests in 1964 initiated secret and unofficial research in 1968 and 1970 (known as the *1968/70 Internal Report*) on the desirability and feasibility of Japan acquiring nuclear weapons.

Against the backdrop of the first North Korean nuclear crisis in 1993–94, the JDA conducted a similar internal review of Japan's nuclear options, producing *A Report Considering the Problems of the Proliferation of Weapons of Mass Destruction* in 1995.[21] Both the 1968/70 and 1995 reports concluded that a nuclear deterrent was neither credible nor necessary for Japan, at least as long as it could rely on the US nuclear umbrella, and that the political, technological and international diplomatic hurdles were too high.[22] Indeed, Japanese policymakers' confidence in the US extended nuclear deterrent proved key in their relatively relaxed response to China's nuclear test in 1964, constant nuclear targeting by the Soviet Union throughout the Cold War, and the North Korean crisis in the mid 1990s.

Japan's initial opposition in 1993 to the indefinite extension of the Nuclear Non-Proliferation Treaty (NPT), combined with its extensive stockpiles of plutonium from civilian reactors (estimated at close to 50 tonnes in 2005), raised fresh questions about its nuclear stance, although in reality Japan's doubts about NPT extension have mainly been related to the effects on peaceful nuclear development and the preservation of the status of the existing nuclear powers.[23] In 1999, Shingo Nishimura, then-parliamentary vice-minister of the JDA and a well known right-winger, was famously dismissed for suggesting that Japan's failure to consider the acquisition of nuclear weapons left it vulnerable to international 'rape'. In April 2002, Ichiro Ozawa, at the time leader of the Liberal Party, reported that, in a recent trip to Beijing, he had told Chinese leaders that 'If Japan desires, it can possess thousands of nuclear warheads. Japan has enough plutonium in use at its nuclear plants for three to four thousand ... If that should happen, we wouldn't lose [to China] in terms of military strength.'[24] In May and June 2002, in response to direct questions on the issue, then-Chief Cabinet Secretary Fukuda and Deputy Chief Cabinet Secretary Abe restated the government's position that Japan had no intention of developing nuclear weapons, but that doing so would not be unconstitutional. Prime Minister Koizumi then moved to smother debate by stating in June 2002 that 'Japan was never going to change its non-nuclear policy'.[25]

Abe's accession to the premiership added fresh impetus to the debate because he was known to be advised by figures such as Terumasa Nakanishi, a Kyoto University professor in favour of actively debating a Japanese nuclear option, and Hisahiko Okazaki, Director of the Okazaki Institute, a former ambassador and known proponent of nuclear weapons for Japan.[26] Abe's arrival in the premiership, and the run-up to the North Korean nuclear test, also coincided with the release in September 2006 of a report on national strategy by the Institute for International Policy Studies (IIPS), a think-tank chaired by former Prime Minister Yasuhiro Nakasone. The IIPS advocated continual and thorough studies of Japan's nuclear option in response to the international situation, while still preserving the Three Non-Nuclear Principles.[27]

By November 2006, Abe had effectively closed down the debate on Japan's nuclear options, and it has stayed closed during Fukuda's and Aso's periods in office. The reasons for Japanese policymakers' reluctance to push the nuclear debate any further at this juncture are essentially the same as in previous years. First, the North Korean nuclear threat is still seen as in its infancy: Pyongyang has yet to develop an effective means to miniaturise its nuclear devices for delivery on ballistic missiles, and the nuclear issue may well be resolved through diplomatic means. Policymakers are also confident that conventional means are sufficient to deter or at least nullify the North Korean threat. BMD offers one way of doing this, and Japan's defence community has considered the use of air power or the acquisition of *Tomahawk* missiles as a means to strike against North Korean missile-launch sites. As Minister of Defense, Ishiba frequently suggested the acquisition of *Tomahawks*, and as JDA director general in 2004 reportedly ordered the National Institute of Defense Studies (NIDS) to look into the feasibility of using cruise missiles to attack North Korean missile bases.[28] Speaking at a Japan–US Security Strategy Conference in Washington DC on 1 May 2007, former JDA Director General Fukushiro Nukaga opined that Japan should debate the acquisition of *Tomahawks* to defend itself and supplement US retaliatory power.[29] A report by the Tokyo Foundation think-tank in October 2008 argued that the MSDF should acquire *Tomahawks* to provide 'deterrence by punishment', to complement the 'punishment by denial' offered by BMD deployment and to strengthen the overall US–Japan deterrence posture.[30]

The second factor in Japan's decision not to seek nuclear weapons is its confidence in the US extended nuclear deterrent. On 19 October 2006, US Secretary of State Rice reiterated the US security guarantee, telling Abe that 'Japan's security is the United States' security'.[31] In December 2006, Aso, despite having earlier contributed to opening the debate on a Japanese nuclear option, expressed his confidence in the solidity of Japan's nuclear arrangements with the US.[32] Japan's continued recourse to the US security guarantee is reinforced by the fact that many policymakers see any attempt to develop an autonomous nuclear option and to break away from the US extended deterrent as exacerbating a potential nuclear arms race in East

Asia, thereby undermining Japan's security. Ishiba summed up this view in November 2006: 'If we develop nuclear weapons, that would be tantamount to saying we don't trust the nuclear deterrence of the United States ... We thereby could make enemies out of both the US and China, which is the scariest scenario.'[33]

Japan's nuclear thinking and freedom of action is further complicated by the plethora of domestic and international legal and other barriers to any deviation from civilian nuclear programmes. Japan imposed constraints on its nuclear policy with the Atomic Energy Basic Law of 1955, which limits nuclear research, development and usage to peaceful purposes. Sato's Three Non-Nuclear Principles were followed in 1968 by the enunciation of the Four Nuclear Policies: the promotion of peaceful nuclear energy, global disarmament, reliance on the US extended nuclear deterrent and support for the Three Non-Nuclear Principles. Japan's nuclear programmes have been subject to International Atomic Energy Agency (IAEA) monitoring since 1957, reinforced by Japan's signing of the NPT in 1970 and its ratification in 1976. Japan's membership of the Nuclear Suppliers Group (NSG) and Zangger Committee means that it cooperates closely with other countries on non-proliferation measures. In addition, Japan has bilateral civilian nuclear agreements with the US, UK, France, China, Canada and Australia for the supply of nuclear fuels and technology, which would result in the cutting off of energy supplies if Japan sought to divert these resources for military use.[34]

These legal constraints are derived from and have helped to reinforce strong domestic anti-nuclear sentiment. Japanese policymaking opinion concerning a nuclear option reflects and certainly has to take note of deeply embedded anti-nuclear feeling among the Japanese public derived from the experiences of Hiroshima and Nagasaki. Continuing anti-nuclear sentiment at the elite level after the North Korean test was demonstrated by the response to Aso and Nakagawa's remarks on the nuclear debate. On 2 November 2006, the DPJ, Japanese Communist Party, Social Democratic Party of Japan (SDPJ) and People's New Party issued a joint protest and called on Lower House Speaker Yohei Kono to clearly express the chamber's opposition to the remarks.[35] This complaint was followed by a letter to Abe on 9 November demanding Aso's dismissal.[36] Meanwhile, on 5 November the National Diet Affairs Committee chairmen, Toshihiro Nikai of the LDP and Yoshio Urushibara of LDP coalition partner New Komeito, demanded that Nakagawa and Aso refrain from calling for a debate on nuclear weapons.[37] The sensitivity of nuclear affairs was again demonstrated with the reaction to remarks by then-Minister of Defense Kyuma in a speech in Chiba Prefecture on 30 June 2007, to the effect that the United States's use of atomic bombs against Japan in the closing stages of the Second World War 'could not be helped' as it was aimed at preventing the Soviet Union from entering the war against Japan. After a dressing down from Abe, Kyuma handed in his resignation on 3 July following fierce criticism from atomic-bomb survivors and their families.[38] Opinion polls demonstrate that the public remains opposed to nuclear armament for Japan.[39]

Finally, Japanese policymakers are aware of the technological obstacles to achieving a credible, independent second-strike deterrent. Japan's plutonium stockpiles might be suitable for the creation of nuclear warheads, although this would involve considerable technical difficulties and expense. Japan has no experience of nuclear testing, and would have to develop suitable delivery systems. It possesses no long-range bombers, and its H-II civilian rocket is liquid-fuelled and thus would have doubtful utility as a second-strike ballistic missile. The country's tight geographical confines mean that it would probably have to develop a submarine-based deterrent to avoid targeting by enemy first strikes, but Japan has not developed the relevant nuclear-power-plant technologies for its submarines. Moreover, Japan must still develop the full panoply of guidance and command and control systems.[40] Japan's advanced technological capabilities mean that it could overcome these difficulties and produce a useable *force de frappe*, but this would require considerable time and would subject Japan to international criticism in the intervening period. Japan would also risk endangering its alliance with the US, further exposing it to risks of nuclear blackmail in the interim period before producing nuclear weapons. As Shinichi Kitaoka, a member of the Prime Minister's Advisory Group on Defense, has argued, Japan would find it infeasible to produce any type of nuclear deterrent that could substitute for the US extended deterrent and fully serve its national-security needs in a situation of a potential nuclear arms race in East Asia.[41]

Hence, Japan appears committed to its non-nuclear stance as long as it has recourse to diplomatic and conventional deterrent options and, crucially, as long as the US–Japan alliance and extended nuclear deterrent remain in place.[42] In addition, Japan's anti-nuclear stance and technological position, although not absolute bars to nuclearisation, tend to reinforce the status quo in its security policy. Nevertheless, there has been definite slippage in Japan's anti-nuclear stance at the elite level. For a start, discussion of nuclear armament, despite attempts to muzzle the debate in late 2006, is no longer taboo.[43] In contrast to the fate of Nishimura in 1999, Nakagawa and Aso were not reprimanded for their attempts to start a debate on a Japanese nuclear option. Japanese policymakers and many commentators generally seem to be of the opinion that, even if Japan cannot at this stage acquire a nuclear capability, the option of doing so should at least be openly and extensively discussed.

The nuclear option is gaining greater credence in Japan because of growing concerns over the basic strategic conditions that have allowed for nuclear restraint in the past. While Japan's anxieties over North Korea should not be exaggerated, they have nonetheless not been assuaged in the absence of a definite resolution to the nuclear crisis through the Six-Party Talks process. China continues to modernise its nuclear forces, and doubts over the credibility of the US extended deterrent and Washington's general non-proliferation stance are growing. Japanese analysts have questioned whether the US would really risk Los Angeles for Tokyo in a nuclear confrontation with North Korea, and whether the US might abandon Japan as an ally.[44]

Japan fears that the US might fail to hold the line in non-proliferation efforts, not only on the Korean Peninsula but also in South Asia and elsewhere. Japan has expressed concern over the US–India nuclear agreement of 2008, which in effect permits India to maintain its nuclear-weapons-power status in exchange for bringing its civilian nuclear programme under international safeguards, thus threatening to undermine the NPT. During a visit to India in September 2007, Abe refused to endorse explicitly the arrangement. Japanese policymakers have, however, accepted it as a done deal, and approved the NSG's supply of civilian nuclear technology to India. Japan's grudging approval of the agreement, which represents some movement away from its previous doctrinaire adherence to the NPT, can only raise doubts as to how far the US would seek to impede other states seeking to acquire nuclear weapons, and whether Japan might view this as an opportunity to reconsider the utility of acquiring its own nuclear option in a nuclearising world.

The primary instinct of most mainstream Japanese policymakers is certainly to remain a 'recessed' nuclear power and to continue to hedge on the nuclear option, maintaining the threat of nuclearisation in order to maximise leverage with the US, protect Japan, and moderate the nuclear programmes of China and North Korea.[45] Japan has many incentives to continue to rattle the sabre, and the weakening nuclear taboo indicates that there are long-term pressures that could make for more substantive changes in its nuclear posture.

Constitutional revision

The principal brake on Japan's remilitarisation has been and remains its constitution. As outlined in Chapter 1, Article 9 is the point of origin for Japan's exclusively defence-oriented policy, its non-exercise of the right of collective self-defence and a range of anti-militaristic prohibitions. The constitution has certainly not proved an absolute barrier to remilitarisation, given the ability of policymakers to reinterpret and stretch constitutional constraints, and that Japan has been able to build up extensive military forces, strengthen US alliance cooperation and deploy the JSDF on a range of overseas operations. Nevertheless, despite Japanese policymakers' past ingenuity, there are increasing indications that the country is bumping up against the limits of constitutional reinterpretation as a means of dealing with international security demands. As a result, pressure for outright revision is increasing.

Japan has been forced to devise a number of makeshift measures under the present constitution in order to enable JSDF overseas deployments in response to global and regional security crises. Japan's failure to respond to US and international expectations that it make a 'human contribution' during the Gulf War of 1990–91 first led Ozawa, as the then-LDP secretary-general, to enunciate the concept of 'international' (*kokusai-teki anzen hosho*) or 'collective' security (*shudan-teki anzen hosho*). Ozawa's concept of 'collective security' contrasted with collective self-defence in that the latter is an inherent right under Chapter 7, Article 51 of the UN Charter, and can be exercised without UN approval in instances where it is deemed necessary to defend another state or ally as if one's own territory were under attack; the former is derived from earlier articles of Chapter 7, especially Article 43, which stress the exercise of force only if sanctioned by the UN and only for purposes of collective retaliation by UN members against aggression.[46] In turn, Ozawa argued that the Preamble of the constitution, which obliges Japan to strive for an honoured position in international society, and thus for enhanced international cooperation, permits the country to participate in UN-sanctioned and UN-centred multilateral military activity, including full war-fighting, without violating Article 9 (which would also be revised at some point, to make clear Japan's right to maintain military forces for international security cooperation).[47] In mid 1991, Ozawa formed a Special Study Group within the LDP on Japan's Role in International Security, but its findings were ignored as the government shifted the focus of its search for an international security role to passage of the IPCL, which enables the deployment of the JSDF on non-combat UNPKO operations.[48]

In its response to the 11 September attacks, Japan again adopted an elastic approach to the constitution. The country could have followed the US in relying principally on the right of individual self-defence, given that Japanese citizens also died in the attacks, but this might then have mandated the constitutional use of force and an open-ended combat mission. Moreover, Japan, in contrast to Washington's NATO allies, could not invoke the right of collective self-defence. Instead, the preference has been to pass individual time-bound legislation – the ATSML and subsequent RSSML – to enable JSDF non-combat overseas deployments, invoking neither individual self-defence nor collective self-defence, but predicated on relevant UN resolutions. Japan stressed UN resolutions identifying the 11 September attacks as a threat to international peace, and calling on all UN members, including by implication Japan, to counter terrorism. This in turn was linked to the injunction within the Preamble of the constitution, stating Japan's obligation to work with international society for the preservation of peace. Japanese policymakers used a similar method to justify the Iraqi Reconstruction Law, enabling the deployment of the JSDF to Iraq from 2004 to 2008. The law was predicated on extant, if rather weak, UN resolutions; in arguing that the deployment was constitutional, Koizumi chose to cite the constitution's Preamble, rather than Article 9, which up until then had been the starting point for any discussion of JSDF deployments overseas.[49]

Successive Japanese governments have employed constitutional sleight of hand to expand JSDF cooperation in regional contingencies. The government deflected accusations during the revision of the US–Japan Guidelines for Defense Cooperation that logistics missions in support of the US might amount to collective self-defence by insisting that it was possible, even in the midst of a major regional conflict, to draw a line between combat zones involving US deployments and non-combat zones for JSDF logistical deployments, and hence that there was no risk of the JSDF becoming involved in combat. Leaders have also argued that the MSDF can if necessary defend US ships when engaged in refuelling operations on the basis of individual self-defence. In October 2006, then-JDA Director General Kyuma compared Japanese refuelling operations to two companions walking alongside each other; one is mugged, and the other seeks to defend him on the basis that the attack might be directed at both.[50]

Such creative constitutional interpretations have enabled the JSDF to undertake a range of new regional and global missions, while also ensuring that Japan does not over-commit itself to certain forms of action. Nevertheless, policymakers understand that, while expedient, these reinterpretations contain major potential drawbacks over the longer term. Japan's non-exercise of collective self-defence, and the circumventions of this injunction through the ATSML and the Iraqi Reconstruction Law, have imposed cumbersome operational restrictions on the JSDF's cooperation with the US and other states in the field. Furthermore, the de facto collective-security option, although opening up the possibility of a genuine combat role for the JSDF, cannot be the principal basis of Japan's international security role because it is centred on the UN. Thus, while Japan can use the UN to legitimise its support for the US in Afghanistan and Iraq, making too much of the links between the UN and its own security policy might create tensions with the US given American disinclination to allow the UN to constrain its own and its allies' military actions. Hence, in cases where there are no extant UN resolutions, the collective-security option might lead to inaction and undermine the bilateral alliance.

Japanese policymakers' dissatisfaction with the limitations of current constitutional restrictions and with the utility of incremental reinterpretations as a means to respond to international crises has been reinforced by a range of emerging security challenges. In particular, policymakers face growing demands from the US to expand regional and global security cooperation, alongside the increased strategic and tactical integration of the JSDF and the US military, raising questions about Japan's future ability to resist pressure to engage in operations in support of the US which might transgress the injunction against collective self-defence. Most significantly, BMD cooperation, underlined by the BMD-related changes in the DPRI and calls from the US for Japan's BMD system to function for the defence of the US homeland, is placing severe stress on the ban on collective self-defence. Japan's government, in moving forward with BMD deployments, has sought to avoid any appearance of a breach of the ban. Announcing in December 2003 Japan's decision to introduce BMD, Fukuda, as chief cabinet secretary, stated that the system

> will be operated on Japan's independent judgement, and will not be used for the purpose of defending third countries. Therefore, it does not raise any problems with regard to the issue of the right of collective self-defence. The BMD system requires interception of missiles by Japan's own independent judgement based on the information on the target acquired by Japan's own sensors.[51]

Japan maintains that any information exchanges with the US for BMD purposes will not necessarily conflict with existing prohibitions on collective self-defence, as they can be classified as routine information-gathering, and not directed specifically to the exercise of the use of force in support of an ally.[52] Japan has deflected US calls for the system to operate in defence of the US homeland by arguing that its current BMD capabilities are technologically insufficient to intercept missiles heading for the US. On 21 November 2006, Kyuma told a press conference that the issue of collective self-defence could not arise because Japan's BMD was 'physically incapable' (*butsuri-teki ni muri*) of pursuing missiles targeted at third countries.[53] He repeated this line in response to criticism by US Secretary of Defense Gates of Japan's stance in bilateral talks in May 2007.[54]

In their efforts to maintain the ban on the exercise of collective self-defence, Japanese policymakers have constructed a second line of argument that maintains the formal prohibition, while at the same time leaving open the possibility of assisting in defending the US from missile attacks if doing so is deemed necessary to preserve the US–Japan alliance. Even though Japanese policymakers are cognisant of the risks of exercising the right of collective self-defence, they are also aware that, if Japan is seen to be totally passive despite possessing an increasing capacity to intercept missiles targeted at the US, this might prove fatal to alliance cooperation. Policymakers have again sought a fallback hedging position, utilising convoluted constitutional interpretation and linguistic artifice. Thus, in 2006 the JDA argued that Japan might act to intercept missiles heading towards the US on the basis that they were passing through Japanese airspace and could jettison debris over Japanese territory, posing a risk to national security and mandating a BMD intercept predicated on the right of individual self-defence.[55]

In the case of BMD, Japanese policymakers have managed to devise a short-term escape route on the issue of collective self-defence and the defence of the US homeland. However, the complex and operationally deficient nature of this position is clearly not satisfactory over the long term, and has not relieved the pressure for reconsideration of the right of collective self-defence as the BMD project progresses. Indeed, Japan's management of collective self-defence issues raised by BMD highlights the fact, for government and opposition alike, that Japan cannot continue to articulate security policy based on constant reinterpretation of its constitution, and consequently that more formal constitutional revision is necessary. As Masazuki Gotoda of the LDP commented at the time of the ATSML debate, the constitution was akin to an 'elastic band' strained to breaking point.[56]

The first moves towards constitutional revision came in April 2005, when the two houses of the National Diet released separate reports on the issue. The House of Representatives reported a consensus that Article 9 should be revised in such a way that the first clause, on the renunciation of the right of belligerency, should be kept in place, but that in the second clause Japan's right of self-defence and the constitutionality of the JSDF should be explicitly acknowledged.[57] The House of Councillors failed to agree on revisions to Article 9, and neither chamber was able to reach consensus on revisions relating to the exercise of the right of collective self-defence, although they both agreed that Japan should engage more actively in international security cooperation.[58] In this sense, many of the changes debated in the Diet reports were only proposals for de jure confirmation of the de facto reality of Japan's security policy. Nonetheless, they were important in initiating more detailed debates on constitutional revision, and in preparing the way for concrete proposals.

As the governing party, the LDP has been the principal instigator of attempts to revise the constitution, and has long advocated formal revision (*kaiken*) as part of its platform. In March 2004, the LDP's Defense Policy Studies Subcommittee issued a report entitled *Recommendations on Japan's New Defense Policy*. This proposed that Japan should amend Article 9 to recognise the JSDF as a national armed force responsible for territorial defence and the support of international security, and to state clearly that Japan possessed the rights of individual and collective self-defence. In addition, the PRC recommended that Japan pass a Basic Law for National Defense and a general law governing international peace-cooperation activities (the forerunner of the permanent dispatch law (*kokyu hoan*)), to replace the existing practice of passing ad hoc legislation to cover individual JSDF missions.[59]

The LDP's New Constitution Drafting Committee (*Shinkempo Kiso Iinkai*) released a draft revision in November 2005, to coincide with the 50th anniversary of the LDP's founding. The draft settled on a number of key issues relating to security.

First, Chapter 2 of the constitution was to be renamed 'security' instead of the 'renunciation of war', with the first paragraph and its pacifist principles retained. Second, the sentence beginning 'in order to' was to be removed and major changes made to the second paragraph acknowledging unambiguously for the first time Japan's right to maintain military forces. The nomenclature of the JSDF was changed, from 'Japan Self Defense Forces' (*Jieitai*) to 'Japan Self Defense Military' (*Jieigun*). The *Jieigun* was specifically charged with international cooperation for the preservation of peace and security. This change was reinforced by a revised Preamble, which stated that the Japanese people pledged to cooperate for the preservation of international peace.[60]

In conjunction with these proposals for formal revision, the LDP sought to tackle the related issue of collective self-defence, not through the process of constitutional revision itself, but through the legislative process via a separate Basic National Security Law that would specify the right of collective self-defence and the particular conditions for its exercise.[61] The LDP believed that it could effect this legislative change because of the subtle modification in the status of the JSDF created by its designation as a military (*gun*) in the revised Article 9. The LDP argued that, by establishing in the constitution the principle of Japan's possession of a military with international security responsibilities, rather than just a force designed for its own national defence alone, and by setting this alongside the already established principle of Japan's inherent possession of the right of collective self-defence, it would be possible to push forward the concept that it is only 'natural' (*tozen*) for Japan to breach its self-imposed ban to exercise this right and to utilise its military forces in support of the US and the wider international community.[62] LDP policymakers appeared confident that this legislative and reinterpretative package could be pushed through the National Diet because the drafting of the bill would enable the party and its New Komeito coalition partner to negotiate acceptable limits on the extent of collective self-defence in terms of specific conditions and geographical extent, and because a straight legislative bill would only require a simple majority in the Diet, rather than the two-thirds majority required to revise the constitution.[63]

The LDP also believed that it shared common ground with the DPJ on constitutional change. The DPJ has followed the LDP in recognising the need for a full debate on the constitution in order to respond to Japan's changing security circumstances, although it has found it harder to develop a party consensus on what form revision should take, and how the party should position itself on the issue vis-à-vis the LDP. The DPJ initiated its own Research Committee on the Constitution in 1999, which produced a mid-term 'proposal' (*teigen*) in June 2004, and a final proposal report in October 2005. The DPJ originally intended to produce its draft version of a new constitution by mid 2006, although as of early 2009 this had yet to materialise. The party's basic position in opposition to the LDP's revision (*kaiken*) is conceptualised as one of constitutional 'augmentation' (*soken*). Influential figures from all wings of the party are disturbed by what they perceive as the 'hollowing out' (*kudoka*) of the constitution's principles by endless government reinterpretations. Instead, the DPJ's basic aim is to augment the fundamental pacifist principles of the constitution and to make a clearer distinction between the use of Japanese military force for individual self-defence and in support of the US, while at the same time expanding Japan's scope for international security cooperation with the wider East Asian regional community and the UN.

In practice, achieving a consensus within the DPJ on advancing constitutional revision has been difficult due to internal factionalism. The SDPJ rump led by Takahiro Yokomichi has opposed revision in general, and especially any moves to lift the prohibition on the exercise of collective self-defence.[64] DPJ President Ozawa has made common cause with Yokomichi on this, arguing that, in line with his notion of collective security, constitutional revision is not necessary to enable Japan to play an international security role. Ozawa and Yokomichi have jointly argued that Japan should thus avoid any changes that would enable the LDP to further expand support for the US, and that instead it should seek to support the establishment of a UN standing army, with JSDF participation.[65] The social progressives in the party, led by former DPJ President Naoto Kan, have maintained a more open mind on revision, while proposing the establishment of a special reserve force, separate from the JSDF, for overseas operations.[66] The intent of Kan and his supporters is to expand the scope for international security cooperation, but to do so in a way divorced from, and therefore limiting the future potential of, JSDF dispatch overseas in support of US military operations in the name of 'international security cooperation'.

Elsewhere in the party there is greater appetite for constitutional revision and the possible exercise of collective self-defence. Former DPJ leader Yukio Hatoyama has advocated a limited form of collective self-defence.[67] Another former leader, Katsuya Okada, caused controversy within the party when he argued in a speech in the US in July 2004 that, based on clear UN resolutions, Japan could use military force to contribute to international security, although this definition was closer to Ozawa's collective-security concept.[68] A third former party chief, Seiji Maehara, has gone further, stating that Japan should, through formal constitutional revision, exercise the right of collective self-defence, and was entitled to use military force in carefully designed circumstances, such as regional contingencies and in UN-led operations.[69] Maehara has emphasised in the past his willingness to work on a bipartisan basis with the LDP on key security legislation and constitutional revision.

These internal divisions within the DPJ have compelled it to forge compromises in its proposals for constitutional revision, as seen in the *teigen* reports of 2004 and 2005. The DPJ, like the LDP, first proposed that the existence of the JSDF and the right of individual self-defence be recognised in the constitution. Its second proposal also focused on specifying an international security role for the JSDF, but this is linked more strongly to the concept of collective security and operations under UN mandates. The extent of force available in these missions was left deliberately vague to placate the party's left wing.[70] The DPJ's third major proposal was to create a Basic Security Law that would set specific restrictions on the international security operations open to the JSDF.[71]

Although the LDP was aware of the not-insignificant challenges to changing the constitution, under the leadership of Abe it began in 2006–07 to press ahead with concrete steps for revision. During his election campaign to become LDP president and Japanese prime minister, Abe made clear his intention to seek constitutional revision, and after securing election duly made this official policy. Abe himself viewed revision of the constitution and the exercise of the right of collective self-defence as an essential part of his vision, in which Japan escapes from the constraints imposed by the post-war settlement (*sengo dakkyaku*) and reasserts its identity as a great power.[72]

Abe subsequently put forward legislation in the National Diet, mooted since Koizumi's period in office, designed to create the procedures for a national referendum on the constitution. Abe was undoubtedly emboldened by his inheritance from Koizumi of a two-thirds 'super-majority' in the House of Representatives (Article 96 of the constitution allows for revision in the case of a two-thirds majority in both chambers, followed by a simple majority in a special referendum), and succeeded in pushing the legislation through the House of Representatives and House of Councillors on 12 April and 14 May 2006. The legislation included a three-year moratorium on attempts to submit drafts for constitutional revision to the Diet. The LDP's intention during this three-year period was to lay the foundations for a bid to revise the constitution, encouraging the formation of a Research Commission on the Constitution in the House of Councillors in January 2007 and a Deliberative Council on the Constitution in the House of Representatives in August 2007, and producing an outline draft for a revised constitution for submission to and passage through the National Diet in 2011. This would be followed by a referendum in the same year.[73]

In the meantime, Abe turned his attention to loosening the restrictions on the exercise of collective self-defence. In an interview with the *Washington Post* on 14 November 2006, he said that, in reaction to US demands, Japan should reconsider the ban on the exercise of the right of collective self-defence to enable it to intercept missiles targeted at the US.[74] This was followed by indications on 20 November from Yasuhisa Shiozaki, then-Chief Cabinet Secretary, that Japan's government might reconsider Fukuda's 2003 statement on BMD, thereby sparking the speculation that necessitated Kyuma's explanation that Japan could not intercept US-bound missiles with its current technological capacities.[75] On 17 April 2007, Abe established a Council on Reconstruction for the Legal Basis for Security within the Prime Minister's Office, chaired by Shunji Yanai, a former ambassador to the US. The panel was charged with researching means of bringing Japan's legal measures into line with a range of new security scenarios facing the JSDF, implicitly including areas where Japan might consider exercising the right of collective self-defence in relation to BMD. Abe's intention to use the panel as a means of whittling away at existing interpretations, thereby building pressure for a breach of the ban, was made clear by the fact that he filled it with experts already known to be supporters of the exercise of collective self-defence.[76]

The Yanai Panel produced its final report on 24 June 2008. It looked at Japan's legal position in four major scenarios: a response to an attack on nearby US warships engaged in joint exercises with the MSDF in international waters; the use of BMD assets to intercept a missile targeted at the US, irrespective of existing technological capabilities; the use of force to defend military personnel of other states engaged in UNPKO operations in which Japan was also participating; and the provision of logistical support to the armed forces of other states involved in UNPKO operations which might involve the use of force.

The panel concluded that, in the first and second scenarios, Japan had no other option but to exercise the right of collective self-defence. In the first, it argued that any attempts to justify Japanese defence of US warships as an act of individual self-defence under Article 95 of the JSDF Law, on the grounds that an attack might also inflict damage on MSDF forces nearby, could only create operational uncertainties and would only apply if the US warships concerned were very close by.[77] The report thus sketched out the possibility that the JSDF might have to sit idly by while its ally's warships suffered damage. In the second scenario, the panel concluded that attempts to justify intercepting a missile targeted at the US as an act of individual self-defence based on Articles 82-2 and 93-3 of the JSDF Law relating to BMD, and drawing on the right to police the safety of the seas, would again founder on a lack of operational clarity. The report pointed out that taking no action would undermine the purpose of BMD in promoting US–Japan alliance cooperation, the US deterrence posture around Japan and the foundations of the alliance. The report stressed that Japan must exercise the right of collective self-defence for operations involving BMD assets deployed on its own territory and in international waters in order to defend the US, though it also noted, though less prominently, that this did not oblige Japan to exercise the same right to defend the US against missile attacks in the territorial waters of other states, thus maintaining some limits on the extent of US–Japan BMD operational commitments outside Japan itself.[78]

As for the third and fourth scenarios, the panel concluded that responses could be possible, not through collective self-defence, but through constitutional reinterpretations utilising individual self-defence. The panel argued that Japan's use of force in support of military personnel from other states involved in UNPKO operations should not be seen as a violation of Article 9's renunciation of the use of force for settling international disputes, as these missions were not traditional wars but UN-mandated operations for the restoration and maintenance of international peace. Similarly, for the fourth scenario, the panel argued that the provision of logistical support to UNPKO was not the same as the use of force in traditional war-fighting, and thus did not transgress Article 9. Indeed, the panel argued, Japan's enhanced participation in scenarios three and four would bring it more closely into line with international norms on the use of force.[79] At the same time, however, the panel did not follow Ozawa in arguing for full collective security, stressing that Japan should only participate selectively in UN peacekeeping operations as its national interests dictated, and that its arguments for reinterpretation did not imply that Japan should as yet engage in full combat duties under UN auspices.[80] Finally, the panel concluded, if Japan was to face squarely the security challenges of the new century, it would have to revisit issues of collective self-defence and constitutional reinterpretation.[81]

Abe's promotion of legislation enabling a national referendum and his institution of the Yanai Panel appeared to signal his administration's intent to move ahead with constitutional change through a combination of formal revision and reinterpretation, broadly in line with LDP policy. However, Abe's plans were derailed by late 2007. The LDP and DPJ were already at loggerheads over whether a special referendum could be used to seek public approval on other policy matters, and whether government employees such as university professors and high-school teachers should be allowed to engage in constitutional debates in the event of a referendum. However, Abe's use of strong-arm tactics to force the referendum legislation through the National Diet, ignoring calls for bipartisanship, only galvanised the DPJ into more active opposition.[82] Abe's tactics also raised concerns within his New Komeito coalition partner, which declared in April and May 2007 that it remained broadly opposed to the exercise of collective self-defence, although it was prepared to tolerate the Yanai Panel's research into 'grey-zone' areas where the distinction between collective and individual self-defence was unclear.[83]

Abe's stance also attracted criticism from the LDP itself, with senior figures stating their discomfort at the prime minister's attempt to introduce collective self-defence through the back door, utilising the Yanai Panel to avoid open debate. Meanwhile, Ishiba compared Abe's tactics to those of his grandfather, Prime Minister Nobusuke Kishi, who forced the revised US–Japan security treaty through the National Diet in 1960.[84] Abe then made the fatal mistake of attempting to campaign on the issue of constitutional revision in the September 2007 elections for the House of Councillors, only to find himself punished by an electorate baffled as to why he was concentrating primarily on this and other foreign-policy issues when the problems of growing economic inequality in Japanese society seemed far more pressing.

Abe's consequent fall from power and the succession of Fukuda further choked off debate on revising the constitution. Fukuda's preoccupation with domestic political and economic problems, scandals in the Ministry of Defense and the maintenance of the MSDF mission in the Indian Ocean meant that he had little appetite for engaging in controversy over the constitution. Indeed, during Fukuda's period in office the Yanai Panel was never convened, and he received its final report in June 2008 with minimal interest and with no intention to act upon it.[85]

As prime minister, Aso has begun to show renewed interest in the exercise of collective self-defence in line with his more assertive stance on security. After speaking at the UN General Assembly in New York on 25 September 2008, just a day after his appointment as prime minister, Aso remarked in response to reporters' questions concerning current constitutional interpretations that collective self-defence was an 'important issue', thereby raising speculation that he might follow Abe in seeking to exercise this right.[86] Foreign Minister Hirofumi Nakasone and Minister of Defense Yasukazu Hamada both denied on 30 September that there were any government moves to change the interpretations relating to collective self-defence, although both were personally in favour of the exercise of this right.[87] However, Aso back-pedalled on his earlier statements on constitutional reinterpretation, stating on 4 November that he had no intention of following this line, undoubtedly mindful of the controversy brewing over Tamogami's essay and issues of civilian control.[88]

Aso's caution has been reinforced by the fact that support for constitutional revision among the Japanese public appears to be falling away. In an *Asahi Shimbun* poll in 2004, 53% of respondents were in favour of revision – the first time a majority had been recorded since the newspaper began polling on the issue. According to the survey, 60% of respondents opposed revision of Article 9, a decline of 14 points from the previous survey in 2001.[89] Another *Asahi Shimbun* poll in 2006 showed that support for constitutional revision had risen overall to 55%; those opposed to revision of Article 9 had dropped to 42%, with those in favour edging ahead for the first time, at 43%, with 15% undecided.[90] Another poll by the newspaper in 2007 recorded 58% in favour of overall constitutional revision, but opponents of any revision of Article 9 had risen to 49%, and those in favour had fallen to 33%, with 18% undecided.[91] In 2008, the same poll suggested that public support had shifted significantly, with 59% opposed to constitutional revision overall, and 66% opposed to revision of Article 9, 23% in favour and 11% undecided.[92] Polls by the *Yomiuri Shimbun* newspaper in 2006 found that 39% were in favour of revising Article 9; by 2007, this had fallen to 36%.[93]

In early 2009, therefore, it appeared that constitutional change, either by formal revision or reinterpretation, has been pushed down the list of Japanese policymakers' security priorities. Nonetheless, Japanese politics remains in the grip of pro-revision LDP politicians, and even if the DPJ gained power its younger members would be keen to move forward on the issue. In March 2008, LDP, DPJ and New Komeito politicians formed a cross-party Dietmen's Alliance for the Establishment of a New Constitution, the 191 National Diet members of which included prominent politicians such as then-LDP Secretary-General Bunmei Ibuki, Makoto Koga, Sadakazu Tanigaki, DPJ Secretary-General Yukio Hatoyama and Seiji Maehara. Japanese security experts also continued to agitate for constitutional revision; Shinichi Kitaoka and Akihiko Tanaka, two of the members of the Yanai Panel, supervised the production of the Tokyo Foundation's October 2008 report on Japan's future security strategy, which called for the exercise of collective self-defence in BMD and international peace operations.[94] Moreover, public opinion, although currently ill-disposed towards constitutional revision and preferring the government to focus instead on domestic economic problems, remains fluid and amenable to consideration of the issue, rather than firmly entrenched against revision as in the past. Finally, Japan's international and domestic security circumstances are likely to stimulate the debate once again. Increased security cooperation with the US in BMD and other operations will lay bare the mounting contradictions and limitations of constant reinterpretation. Hence, Japanese policymakers will continue to chip away at resistance to constitutional revision, and may move more radically should Japan face new crises highlighting the untenable nature of Article 9 and its related restrictions on the exercise of military power.

Military education, patriotism and attitudes towards the use of military force

Japan's remilitarisation depends not only on the removal of the formal constitutional barriers to the use of force, but also upon a deeper acceptance among the Japanese population of the necessity and efficacy of a more proactive security policy and, ultimately, of the use of force for national security ends.

Japan's most influential policymakers have embarked on a campaign to educate the public about the importance of national security, and to reach out to a wider audience among different sections of the population. The Ministry of Defense, in addition to its extensive, 400-page-plus annual *Defense of Japan* White Paper, has since 2005 produced a 'compact' version of around half the size to make defence policy intelligible to a broader readership. A manga cartoon version is also produced, again designed to explain in simple terms, and presumably to a younger audience, recent developments in defence policy. Another manga aims to educate the public about BMD.

These efforts are notable, not only for portraying Japan as highly vulnerable to external threats, but also in juxtaposing images of threat with the determined and teamlike efforts of manga characters, and by association the JSDF, to defend the nation. Hence, in the 2005 manga version of the *Defense of Japan* one of the central characters is a naïve, 'peace-loving' teddy bear, who comes to learn of and bemoan the security realities that Japan faces, before then duly becoming reassured as to Japan's security by the efforts of the JSDF.[95] Meanwhile, in the BMD manga the two main characters are a boy and girl who, in a narrative intertwined with their pastime of playing with and supporting their soccer team, learn about the perils of missile attacks and the benefits of missile defence. The missile threats other countries such as North Korea pose to Japan are likened in the story to the problem of players in a soccer match facing a mismatch when they employ fair play in the face of illegal and underhanded tactics, while the use of BMD is likened to a new form of defensive organisation on the soccer pitch.[96] The Ministry of Defense and the JSDF also cooperated with publishers to produce the magazine *Securitarian* until 2005, again designed to educate the public about the activities of the JSDF, and now sponsor the publication of a similar magazine, *Mamoru* (*Defend*).

Other influential opinion-formers have also been working to educate the public concerning defence. After his first stint as defence minister, Ishiba produced a set of polemical memoirs and a manga introductory text to Japan's defence policy, the latter containing a variety of apocalyptic scenarios including a successful North Korean nuclear-armed ballistic-missile attack on Japan, and an attempt by terrorists to hijack a Japanese domestic flight and crash it into a nuclear-power station.[97]

Japan's bookshops are perceptibly fuller today than at any time in the past with a range of texts by academics, retired bureaucrats and politicians that urge the need for the public to learn about the dangers surrounding Japan and the intricacies of national security policy. In addition, less sober publications designed to appeal to the more casual reader and *gunji otaku* (that is, those with a stay-at-home, obsessive interest in military affairs) have become increasingly bold in outlining threat scenarios such as a Chinese military clash with Japan, and in expressing desires for Japan to acquire stronger military power, including aircraft carriers and stealth fighters.[98]

Japanese policymakers and other writers are in many cases simply seeking to educate the population in a serious manner about issues of security policy. But the growing depth of the material on security policy seems to suggest that the issue is no longer taboo, and in some cases there is a sense in which education about military matters in more popular and even serious material has begun to spill over into celebrating the role of the military and the potential use of force. Moreover, evidence from government opinion polls suggests that there is growing acceptance among the Japanese public of the need for education in military affairs, not just in official literature and commercial publications, but also in the education system itself. According to these polls (see Appendix: Chart 8), those supporting teaching regarding national defence in places of education had risen to almost 70% by 2006. This suggests an increasing consensus that Japan should address more squarely throughout society and as part of the educational curriculum the previous taboo issue of security.

The indications are that Japanese policymakers would like to exploit this sentiment to develop not just general education about security matters but also education grounded in stronger forms of 'patriotism' and the duty to defend the state. Early LDP drafts for a new constitution included a stipulation that Japanese citizens had an obligation to defend their country. Although the final draft watered down these provisions, it supplemented the existing constitution's provisions relating to Japan's trust in the capacity of the peace-loving peoples of the world to achieve international peace with the injunction that the Japanese people would now 'resolve to maintain their own security and existence'.[99]

The LDP's interest in inculcating a sense of patriotic duty to defend the nation has been further manifested in revisions of the Fundamental Law of Education passed in December 2006. The original 1947 law was part of a package of Occupation democratisation and demilitarisation reforms, and conservative politicians have long objected to it as imposing 'alien values' on Japan, and dislike its lack of provision for patriotic education, the conception of the state and observance of the national anthem and flag. After considerable debate with opposition parties over how to define patriotism, the LDP succeeded in inserting into the revised law a clause that required the education system 'to foster a disposition to respect Japanese culture and tradition, love the country and homeland that nurtured them, together with respect for other countries and a desire to contribute to world peace and the development of the international community'.[100]

The LDP's reintroduction of patriotic education was made palatable by additional statements promoting international cooperation. But the intent of conservative politicians to strengthen a sense of duty to the state among individual citizens was unmistakable, and represented a radical change given post-war Japan's attempts to avoid patriotism in the education system as one of the key means to deracinate militarism. Indeed, for one observer the revised Fundamental Law on Education is seen to parallel or even exceed the laws of pre-war Japan in advancing patriotic education.[101] Most notably, the Imperial Rescript on Education of 1890, one of the foundational documents of the modern Japanese state, contains only the vague stipulation that subjects would offer themselves 'courageously to the state', with no mention of love of country. The Rescript was repealed under the Occupation because of its perceived role in promoting militarism.[102]

Finally, in addition to plans for constitutional change and the revision of the Fundamental Law on Education, the government in 1999 implemented the Law Concerning the National Flag and Anthem, which designated the Hinomaru and Kimigayo – two of the most prominent symbols of pre-war Japanese militarism – as the nation's official flag and anthem. All of these measures taken together may be interpreted as efforts to foster a legitimate sense of patriotism, but they also represent attempts to reverse many of the steps taken to demilitarise Japan in the post-war period, and raise questions about the dividing-line between so-called 'healthy patriotism', nationalism and remilitarisation.

Japan's remilitarisation will take its most significant form, however, at the point at which its policymakers and citizens come to accept the use of force as a legitimate and effective means of ensuring national security ends, thus representing a turning away from the anti-militaristic principles embedded in Japanese society in the post-war period. The signs in recent years are that, while Japan is still a long way from losing its ingrained suspicion of the use of force, it is progressively inching towards a greater degree of acquiescence in the need to employ its own military capabilities and to support the military efforts of the US and other states to achieve national and international security objectives.

Japan has certainly demonstrated a greater degree of acceptance of the need not only to build its own defensive capabilities to deter aggression against its national territory, but also to use these capabilities proactively if necessary, while at the same time reinforcing the US–Japan alliance as the other key basis of Japan's security. As noted earlier, in the eyes of the public the JSDF has gained legitimacy as the body responsible for the defence of Japan itself. Similarly, Japanese support for the US alliance has grown since the 1980s, with those viewing it as functioning effectively for Japan's security rising to a high of 75% by 2006 (see Appendix: Chart 9). Public approval of a combination of the JSDF and the US–Japan security treaty as the best means to ensure national security has risen, from 40% in the 1970s to close to 80% in 2006. Meanwhile, support for other options, such as Japan defending itself independently or seeking an unarmed posture, has remained marginal (Chart 10). Japanese opinion over the last 20 years or so has thus become more comfortable with a national defence posture reliant upon a combination of the JSDF and US–Japan security cooperation, and by implication can be said to have become comfortable with the constant strengthening of the capabilities and ambitions of the JSDF and the US alliance over the same period. Despite the constant upgrading of the functional and geographical capabilities of the alliance and the possible risks accompanying this process, support for it has only increased.

These changes have been matched by a new willingness to move beyond deterrence and to deploy military power to repel aggression. Japan's response to incursions by North Korean spy ships demonstrates this increased acceptance of the legitimate use of force. The government reacted to the incursion of a North Korean spy ship into Japan's territorial waters in March 1999 by permitting JSDF ships to fire a total of 35 warning shots, and two P-3Cs dropped four 150kg bombs as a warning. These were the first shots fired in anger by Japan's civilian or military forces since the Maritime Safety Agency (MSA) (the forerunner of the JCG) attempted to intercept a ship believed to be rendezvousing with Soviet agents off the coast of Hokkaido in 1953. Japan went a step further in December 2001, permitting the paramilitary JCG to sink a North Korean spy ship, claiming the lives of ten members of its crew. This was the first use of lethal force by the Japanese state in the post-war period, and the interception and sinking of the ship received widespread public support as a necessary means of defending Japanese territory. The use of force in this case should not be exaggerated, as it was arguably proportionate and directed through the JCG rather than the JSDF. Nevertheless, it was an important breach of the normative restrictions on the use of defensive military power in Japan, and creates a precedent for similar acts in the future.

This coming to terms with the use of military capabilities for immediate national defence has not yet been matched by greater certainty in the deployment of the JSDF overseas, or unequivocal support for the US's exercise of military force in international security contingencies outside the Asia-Pacific region. From polling evidence, Japan's population can be said to distinguish between 'defensive' and 'offensive' wars.[103] The Japanese public thus proved generally more supportive of the war in Afghanistan, which it viewed as a clear defensive response to terrorist threats to the US and the international community, but grew increasingly ambivalent about the war in Iraq and regime change there, which were perceived as more offensive in nature.[104] Consequently, Japanese public opinion helped to set the parameters of the Japanese government's provision of support for the US in these conflicts, and in influencing the form in which the JSDF was deployed. Japanese policymakers were aware that public opinion would not accept any operation which might be seen to breach constitutional prohibitions, hence reinforcing their intent to deploy the JSDF in a non-combat role to support the US and international coalitions. In this sense, public opinion can be seen to have been a brake upon external remilitarisation.

It is not, however, an *absolute* brake, either in terms of Japan's use of its own military power overseas, or in terms of its support for the projection of US military power. The Japanese public may not support JSDF deployments in overseas operations that are perceived as offensive in nature, but the wars in Afghanistan and to a lesser extent Iraq demonstrate that they are prepared to accept JSDF operations in these conflicts provided they are portrayed as non-combat missions. More importantly, it is clear that, even if the Japanese public is unenthusiastic about dispatching the JSDF to support apparently offensive military operations, it is not opposed to facilitating the projection of US offensive military power in these operations. Japan's increasing acceptance of the US–Japan security treaty as bolstering its national security, and the implicit acceptance of the expansion of the functional and geographical scope of alliance cooperation, has already been commented upon. Japanese opinion polls also show that, even though there is increasing recognition of the possibility of Japan becoming embroiled in conflict, mainly as a result of a rise in international tensions and the ineffective functioning of the UN (Charts 11 and 12), the US–Japan security treaty is actually seen as an insurance against such involvement (Chart 13). All of this suggests that Japanese public opinion is relatively comfortable with the expansion of alliance cooperation, and sees minimal risk of entrapment as long as Japan is not involved in combat operations directly alongside the US. In terms of Japan's role in the projection of US military power internationally, this arguably translates into acquiescence in US offensive wars as long as they are not seen to impact directly upon Japan.

The fact that Japanese public opinion accepts this role clearly provides policymakers with the necessary room to stretch interpretations of the US–Japan alliance and to allow the US increasingly to project power beyond Japan's immediate environment and the Asia-Pacific region, as seen in the negotiations over the DPRI. It also provides policymakers with some space to support this global power projection through the JSDF, as long as such missions are not seen as involving combat. Hence, even if Japan cannot be said fully to have overcome its resistance to external militarisation with regard to deploying the JSDF for the use of force overseas, it can be said to have remilitarised externally, if indirectly, through its support for the projection of US military force in offensive wars. In this sense, it is a mistake to argue that Japan's remilitarisation only extends to a new determination to defend its own national territory, and that this process does not apply to attempts to support offensive wars overseas, when Japan has clearly been complicit in the United States's use of offensive force globally.

Conclusion

Japan's formal and normative anti-militaristic principles have gradually been eroded. Japanese society values its military establishment more highly than at any other time in the postwar period. Japan's anti-nuclear taboos are not breached, but neither are they immovable. The issue of constitutional revision has been at the centre of the political agenda, and Japanese policymakers have put in place plans and legislation in readiness for a revision at the appropriate time. Policymakers are currently preoccupied with other, more pressing, issues, and the Japanese public is not enthusiastic about devoting energy to questions of remilitarisation. Nonetheless, the perceived contradictions between Japan's constitution and its security ambitions mean that the issue of revision is likely to return over the longer term. Japan is also growing more tolerant of military and patriotic education, more willing to accept the use of force in defence of the national territory and more supportive of a stronger alliance to support US offensive military power.

CONCLUSION

Japan has continued its long-term trajectory of remilitarisation in the post-Koizumi period. Progress has not been entirely smooth, and has certainly been less eye-catching than during Koizumi's period in office. Nevertheless, judged against objective international criteria, and against its own self-imposed standards, Japan has overcome many barriers to remilitarisation and has strengthened its national and international security profile in a number of key areas.

Japan's strategic environment continues to exert pressure for remilitarisation over the long term. Immediate concerns over North Korea and long-term concerns over China have intensified in the post-Koizumi era, obliging policymakers to continue to rethink defence doctrines and capabilities in order to respond to regional challenges. Japan also faces a range of ongoing global security challenges, alongside emergent alliance demands from the US, obliging it to continue recalibrating its military capabilities and reforming its military-cooperation arrangements with the US.

Japanese military procurement plans reflect this long-term restructuring of capabilities. The defence budget is certainly an important, but not absolute, constraint on further remilitarisation. In de facto terms defence expenditure has exceeded the 1% of GNP ceiling, is flexible enough to allow for major procurement programmes through deferred payments and is growing through 'hidden budgets' for the paramilitary JCG. JSDF procurement priorities are devoted to the pursuit of power projection rather than simple territorial defence, thus breaching another principle constraining militarisation. The GSDF has continued to develop more mobile, rapid-reaction-type capabilities; the ASDF is acquiring new fighters, tankers, transports and munitions to enable it to operate more easily beyond Japanese territory; and the MSDF is concentrating on destroyers, light carriers, amphibious craft and patrol aircraft to project its presence in the Asia-Pacific and well beyond. Japan is moving forward steadily in its long-term project for the deployment of *Aegis* and PAC-3 BMD. The acquisition of IGSs and the Basic Space Law of 2008 mean that Japan has now also breached the ban on the peaceful use of space. Meanwhile, the JCG continues to grow in size and capability. All of these developments strongly complement regional and global functions within the US–Japan alliance.

Japanese remilitarisation has also been marked by a transformation in civil–military relations. The Ministry of Defense and JSDF have gradually elevated their role in the security-policymaking process, and the JSDF has challenged the old system of bureaucratic civilian control in order to gain greater access to the political leadership. In this sense, the Tamogami affair is less a sign of isolated discontent with existing forms of civilian control and more a confirmation of and further trigger to increasing JSDF confidence in its ability to influence defence policy.

Japan has also continued to ease the constraints on the formation of a military-industrial complex. Defence-procurement scandals are not one-off incidents, but arguably manifestations of deepening structural collusion between civilian industry, politicians, bureaucrats and the military. In its search for enhanced technological-development opportunities, Japan's troubled defence industry has begun to create a transnational military-industrial complex with the US. This transnationalisation of defence production has been accompanied by the erosion of Japan's ban on arms export and moves to develop export markets in other parts of the world.

Japan's external commitments have been regarded as the area of greatest retrenchment in the post-Koizumi period. In the face of domestic political opposition, the government has been forced to curtail many of the JSDF's most prominent activities in Iraq and the Indian Ocean. Nevertheless, policymakers have still managed to maintain the mission in the Indian Ocean, and have used the experience of JSDF deployments overseas as a foundation to continue exploring alternative options for cooperation in international coalitions. Japan has not sent the JSDF to Afghanistan, switching instead to anti-piracy missions. In early 2009, Japan thus looked set to increase the size of its MSDF deployments in the Indian Ocean and beyond.

Japan has furthermore been developing links with new external security partners, in particular Australia and India. Nonetheless, the key channel of external remilitarisation has remained the mechanism of US–Japan alliance transformation and realignment. Japan has persevered in the implementation of the DPRI, and through it its support for the enhanced projection of US military power regionally and now globally. US–Japan military cooperation has also been strengthened over the long term through the deployment of BMD and its place within global US missile-defence strategy.

Japanese remilitarisation has also continued in terms of the erosion of domestic anti-militaristic principles. The JSDF has enjoyed growing societal status as a profession and with respect to its responsibilities for national defence and international security cooperation. Japanese anti-nuclearism remains an important constraint on remilitarisation, but has shown signs of weakening in the face of North Korea's nuclearisation. Policymakers have not yet succeeded in revising the constitution, but they have stimulated a long-term debate on the issue and laid the foundations for possible future revision and the exercise of the right of collective self-defence by a mixture of formal legal means and informal reinterpretation. Japanese society now appears more tolerant of military and patriotic education and, most important of all, seems to accept the use of force for national security ends and to acquiesce in the role of the US–Japan alliance in supporting the projection of US offensive power.

Thus, by any measure, Japan has continued on its path of remilitarisation, more-or-less unaffected by political machinations. This has been manifested in long-term changes in the structures of its military capabilities, in civil–military relations, in the military-industrial complex, in Japan's external military commitments and in societal attitudes towards the military and military power. One by one, Japan has transgressed its own key anti-militaristic principles, including the 1% of GNP limit on defence expenditure, the eschewing of power projection, the peaceful use of space, the subordination of the military to civilian authority in security policymaking, the ban on arms exports, the nuclear taboo and constitutional revision. While progress has been slower and has attracted less international attention under Koizumi's successors, it has nonetheless continued.

Japan's remilitarisation: implications and future directions

Japan's incremental, long-term remilitarisation has important implications for regional and global security. Japanese policymakers continue to enhance their military capabilities to respond to North Korea and China. Indeed, Japan is engaged in building up JSDF capabilities to shadow and match China's expanding military power. Japan and China are engaged in a quiet arms-race dynamic, with Japan looking to acquire capabilities to check new Chinese air-defence, blue-water, amphibious and cruise- and ballistic-missile capabilities. Japan is not planning, though, to face down North Korea and China on its own, and its capabilities are increasingly tailored to be interoperable with the US. Hence, the direction of Japan's remilitarisation remains very much in conformity with US–Japan alliance needs, and continues to bolster US regional military hegemony. Japan remains crucial to any attempts by the US to contain North Korea's nuclearisation and the ballistic-missile threat, as shown by US–Japan BMD cooperation in reaction to Pyongyang's projected test in April 2009. Japan also remains the sine qua non for US strategy to manage and counter the rise of China. At the same time, Japan's remilitarisation runs the risk of further stimulating Sino-Japanese rivalry.

Japan's continued ambitions to project power outside its own region also have ramifications for global security. MSDF deployments in the Indian Ocean and Gulf of Aden make Japan an even more important player in global maritime security. Japan's intention is not just to counter transnational terrorism and piracy, but also to lay down a marker of its intent to counter China's rising influence in these areas and to protect its sea lines of communication (SLOC). Just as in the Asia-Pacific region, Japan is developing its global security role in conjunction with changes in the US–Japan alliance. The JSDF is continuing to acquire the necessary capabilities and operational experience to participate in US-led international coalitions, and the transformation of the US–Japan alliance enhances Japan's function as a shield for the sword of

US global power projection. Bilateral cooperation in missile-defence systems further contributes to Japan's integration into US global military strategy. The US–Japan alliance is thus becoming, ever-more substantively and explicitly, an alliance functioning for global security, in support of global US military dominance.

Japan's remilitarisation increases its importance as a US ally, and there appears little prospect that the Obama administration will seek to downgrade security ties. The administration might push Japan less hard on JSDF deployment to theatres such as Afghanistan, thereby demonstrating greater sensitivity to Japan's constitutional limitations than the Bush administration, and a greater awareness of Japan's ability to contribute to international security through 'smart power': a combination of military, economic, diplomatic and 'soft power'. But the administration is just as likely as its predecessor to emphasise continued alliance transformation and realignment to ensure that Japan is better able to defend US capabilities and bases in the Asia-Pacific region, and that Tokyo takes a more flexible approach to US global deployments from Japan to other regions. Japan's importance to the Obama administration was demonstrated by the fact that Tokyo was the destination for new US Secretary of State Clinton's first overseas trip in February 2009, and Aso was the first foreign leader to visit the new president in the White House later the same month. In the first months of the administration, Obama and Clinton repeatedly stated that Japan was the 'cornerstone' of US East Asian security strategy. Moreover, if the 2007 Nye–Armitage report can be taken as at least a partial guide to future US policy towards Japan, pressure from the US is likely to continue for Japan to breach the ban on collective self-defence, to pass a permanent law on dispatching the JSDF and to boost defence expenditure and strengthen ties with US allies.[1]

Remilitarisation might be challenged if the LDP is displaced by the DPJ in National Diet elections scheduled for 2009, or if the DPJ takes power at a later date. DPJ president Ozawa seeks a more equal alliance relationship, with Japan less dependent on the US and consulted more on strategic matters, and looks instead to expand multilateral cooperation with the UN and East Asian states. Ozawa declared in February 2009 that the US strategy to increase troop numbers in Afghanistan was flawed without an accompanying political and economic reconstruction strategy, and that the US military presence in Japan should be reduced, and possibly limited to the Seventh Fleet alone.[2] The DPJ, though, even it were to form an administration, is unlikely to be able significantly to deflect Japan from current and planned levels of alliance cooperation. The strategic environment limits alternative options in East Asia, and Japan's military capabilities and strategy are geared to alliance functions. Moreover, even if the DPJ were to seriously pursue alternative security strategies separate from the US, the result might actually be to remilitarise Japan even more drastically. Ozawa's argument for reduced dependence on the US would probably oblige Japan to boost defence spending substantially and possibly even force serious consideration of the nuclear option, an agenda simply unacceptable to his own coalition partners and public opinion. Meanwhile, Ozawa's concept of collective security might mandate combat operations for the JSDF, a far more radical step than anything envisaged by the LDP, and again a move likely to be unpalatable to the Japanese public.

Japan is, therefore, unlikely to diverge from or backtrack on its current trajectory of remilitarisation, channelled via the US–Japan alliance. The question then becomes how far remilitarisation will advance. It will almost certainly remain incremental, and is only likely to move faster if more assertive leadership emerges domestically, or if a sudden crisis is encountered internationally. Japan is unlikely ever to retread the path of remilitarisation to the point that it tips into militarism akin to that of the pre-war period. Democratic institutions are far too well developed for that, and Japan is likely to be content with eroding and breaching a certain number of anti-militaristic principles to allow it to perform as a more reliable US ally. It is improbable that Japan would ever seek to breach the anti-nuclear principle, for instance. Japan's place within the US alliance is another key contrast with the earlier age of militarisation, and should perform a key role in channelling growing Japanese military ambitions.

At the same time, all parties will need to carefully calibrate their security strategies in response to Japan's more militarised stance. Potential security adversaries in East Asia, including China and North Korea, will need to approach a more militarised Japan with greater caution. These states must ensure that they do not cross certain red lines for Japan's security, such as threatening its SLOC or promoting further WMD proliferation, which might provoke a stronger defensive response from Japan than ever before imaginable in the post-war period. Similarly, the US and other potential new security partners need to recognise the opportunities but also the need for caution in engaging with a remilitarising Japan. The US may seek to nudge Japan towards enhanced security cooperation, but it needs to recognise that Japan is a changing quantity as an alliance partner. Japan will demand increased reciprocity from the US in return for meeting expanding alliance expectations. Since the Bush administration, American 'Japan-handlers' have arguably recognised the need to create a more genuinely equal alliance relationship, under which Japan appears as less a follower and more of a partner.[3] However, the Bush administration found it difficult to manage Japanese expectations with regard to

North Korea and UN Security Council reform. The Obama administration will need to be seen to reciprocate more fully on key strategic issues, including North Korea and China, if it is not to find itself saddled with a more obdurate alliance partner more willing to question US security strategy and to generate tensions with regional neighbours. Other partners, such as NATO, India and Australia, also need to take Japan's great-power status and ambitions seriously, and be willing to support its core security interests, if they wish to engage it as a proper security partner. Finally, Japan itself needs to recognise that its remilitarisation may raise concerns that will need assuaging among its neighbours.

Table 1: **Japanese defence-related expenditures, 1955–2008** (Unit: ¥100 million)

Fiscal year	GNP/GDP (original forecast) (A)	Annual expenditures on General Account (B)	Defence- related expenditures (C) (top figure for each year from 1997 onwards excludes SACO)	Ratio of defence-related expenditures to GNP/GDP (C/A)	Ratio of defence-related expenditures to annual expenditures on General Account (C/B)	Pensions to surviving families and ex-service personnel (D)	Total defence budget calculated on NATO basis (E=C+D)	Ratio of defence-related expenditures to GNP/GDP (E/A)	JCG budget (F)	Total defence budget calculated on NATO basis (G=E+F)	Ratio of defence-related expenditures to GNP/GDP (G/A)	Defence expenditures in US$
1955	75,590	9,915	1,349	1.78	13.61	6,870	8,219	10.8	62	8,281	11.0	N/A
1965	281,600	36,581	3,014	1.07	8.24	13,560	16,574	5.8	154	16,728	6.0	N/A
1975	1,585,000	212,888	13,273	0.84	6.23	12,640	25,913	1.6	638	26,551	1.7	4,484
1985	3,146,000	524,996	31,371	0.997	5.98	15,790	47,161	1.5	1,175	48,336	1.5	14,189
1986	3,367,000	540,886	33,435	0.993	6.18	15,630	49,065	1.5	1,185	50,250	1.5	20,930
1987	3,504,000	541,010	35,174	1.004	6.50	16,070	51,244	1.5	1,224	52,468	1.5	25,420
1988	3,652,000	566,997	37,003	1.013	6.53	15,990	52,993	1.5	1,217	54,210	1.5	28,850
1989	3,987,000	604,142	39,198	1.006	6.49	15,890	55,088	1.4	1,336	56,424	1.4	30,090
1990	4,172,000	662,368	41,593	0.997	6.28	15,810	57,403	1.4	1,326	58,729	1.4	28,122
1991	4,596,000	703,474	43,860	0.954	6.23	15,610	59,470	1.3	1,523	60,993	1.3	32,890
1992	4,837,000	722,180	45,518	0.941	6.30	15,480	60,998	1.3	1,549	62,547	1.3	34,300
1993	4,953,000	723,548	46,406	0.937	6.41	15,440	61,846	1.3	1,642	63,488	1.3	39,710
1994	4,885,0000	730,817	46,835	0.959	6.41	15,400	62,235	1.3	1,559	63,794	1.3	42,100
1995	4,928,000	709,871	47,236	0.959	6.65	15,100	62,336	1.3	1,878	64,214	1.3	53,800
1996	4,960,000	751,049	48,455	0.977	6.45	14,570	63,025	1.3	1,698	64,723	1.3	45,100
1997	5,158,000	773,900	49,414	0.958	6.39							
			49,475	0.959	6.39	14,030	63,505	1.2	1,668	65,173	1.3	42,900
1998	5,197,000	776,692	49,290	0.948	6.35							
			49,397	0.95	6.36	13,540	62,937	1.2	1,864	63,121	1.2	35,200
1999	4,963,000	818,601	49,201	0.991	6.01							
			49,322	0.994	6.03	13,140	62,462	1.3	1,806	64,268	1.3	41,100

Table 1 (cont.): **Japanese defence-related expenditures, 1955–2008** (Unit: ¥100 million)

Fiscal year	GNP/GDP (original forecast) (A)	Annual expenditures on General Account (B)	Defence- related expenditures (C) (top figure for each year from 1997 onwards excludes SACO)	Ratio of defence-related expenditures to GNP/GDP (C/A)	Ratio of defence-related expenditures to annual expenditures on General Account (C/B)	Pensions to surviving families and ex-service personnel (D)	Total defence budget calculated on NATO basis (E=C+D)	Ratio of defence-related expenditures to GNP/GDP (E/A)	JCG budget (F)	Total defence budget calculated on NATO basis (G=E+F)	Ratio of defence-related expenditures to GNP/GDP (G/A)	Defence expenditures in US$
2000	4,989,000	849,871	49,218	0.987	5.79							
			49,358	0.989	5.81	12,750	62,108	1.2	1,790	63,898	1.3	45,600
2001	5,186,000	826,524	49,388	0.952	5.98							
			49,553	0.956	6.0	12,180	61,733	1.2	1,877	63,610	1.2	40,400
2002	4,962,000	812,300	49,395	0.995	6.08							
			49,560	0.999	6.1	11,440	61,000	1.2	1,775	62,775	1.3	39,500
2003	4,986,000	871,891	49,265	0.988	6.02							
			49,530	0.993	6.06	10,830	60,360	1.2	1,730	62,090	1.3	41,600
2004	5,006,000	821,109	48,764	0.974	5.94							
			49,030	0.979	5.97	10,230	59,260	1.2	1,746	61,006	1.2	45,151
2005	5,115,000	821,829	48,301	0.944	5.88							
			48,564	0.949	5.91	9,680	58,244	1.1	1,778	60,022	1.2	43,910
2006	5,139,000	796,860	47,906	0.932	6.01							
			48,139	0.937	6.04	9,070	57,209	1.1	1,919	59,128	1.2	41,144
2007	5,219,000	829,088	47,818	0.916	5.77							
			48,016	0.916	5.79	8,400	56,344	1.07	1,982	58,326	1.12	41,039
2008	5,269,000	830,613	47,426	0.900	5.71							
			47,796	0.907	5.75	N/A	N/A	N/A	N/A	N/A	N/A	N/A

Sources: Ministry of Defense, *Defense of Japan 2008* (Boeishohen, *Boei Hakusho*) (English and Japanese editions); *Boei Handobukku* (Tokyo: Asagumo Shimbunsha, various years); International Institute for Strategic Studies, *The Military Balance* (London: Routledge, various years) (for figures in US dollars); *Japan Statistical Yearbook/Nihon Tokei Nenkan 2008* (Tokyo: Somusho Tokeikyoku, 2008), http://www.stat.go.jp/English/data/nenkan/1431-05.htm (for military pension figures); Kaijo Hoancho Somubu Seimuka (for JCG figures; includes original allocations and revised additions).

Table 2: **Japanese defence budget total accumulated future commitments 1994–2008** (Unit: ¥100 million)

	Total future commitments	Total defence budget	Ratio of future commitments to total defence budget
1994	28,897	46,835	62.0
1995	29,750	47,236	63.0
1996	30,440	48,455	63.0
1997	31,340	49,475	63.5
1998	30,914	49,397	63.0
1999	30,431	49,322	62.0
2000	29,819	49,358	60.4
2001	29,647	49,553	60.0
2002	29,551	49,560	60.0
2003	29,421	49,530	59.4
2004	29,353	49,030	60.0
2005	29,663	48,564	61.1
2006	3,0014	48,139	61.1
2007	29,929	48,016	62.3
2008	30,360	47,796	63.5

Source: Boei Kankokai Henshubu, *Boei Nenkan*, various years

Table 3: **JSDF capabilities at the time of the 1976 and 1995 NDPOs and the 2004 NDPG**

		1976 NDPO	1995 NDPO	2004 NDPG
	GSDF personnel	180,000	160,000	155,000
	Regular personnel		145,000	148,000
	Ready-reserve personnel		15,000	7,000
	Major units			
	Regionally deployed units	12 divisions	8 divisions	8 divisions
		2 combined brigades	6 brigades	6 brigades
GSDF	Mobile operation units	1 armoured division	1 armoured division	1 armoured division
		1 airborne brigade	1 airborne brigade	Central Readiness Group
		1 helicopter brigade	1 helicopter brigade	
	Ground-to-air missile units	8 anti-aircraft artillery groups	8 anti-aircraft artillery groups	8 anti-aircraft artillery groups
	Main equipment			
	Battle tanks	approximately 1,200	approximately 900	approximately 600
	Artillery	approximately 1,000	approximately 900	approximately 600
	Major units			
	Destroyer units (for mobile operations)	4 flotillas	4 flotillas	4 flotillas
	Destroyer units (Regional district units)	10 divisions	7 divisions	5 divisions
MSDF	Submarine units	6 divisions	6 divisions	4 divisions
	Minesweeping units	2 flotillas	1 flotilla	1 flotilla
	Land-based patrol aircraft units	16 squadrons	13 squadrons	9 squadrons
	Main equipment			
	Destroyers	approximately 60	approximately 50	47
	Submarines	16	16	16
	Combat aircraft	approximately 220	approximately 170	approximately 150
	Major units			
	Aircraft control and warning units	28 groups	8 groups	8 groups
		1 squadron	20 squadrons 1 airborne early-warning squadron	20 squadrons
	Interceptor units	10 squadrons	9 squadrons	12 squadrons
ASDF	Support fighter units	3 squadrons	3 squadrons	
	Air-reconnaissance units	1 squadron	1 squadron	1 squadron
	Air-transport units	3 squadrons	3 squadrons	3 squadrons
	Ground-to-air-missiles units	6 groups	6 groups	6 groups
	Main equipment			
	Combat aircraft	approximately 400	approximately 400	approximately 350
	Fighters (included in combat aircraft)	approximately 350	approximately 300	approximately 260

Source: Boeichohen, *Boei Hakusho* (Tokyo: Okurasho Insatsukyoku, 1995), pp. 312, 321; *National Defense Program Guidelines, FY 2005-*, Ministry of Defense, National Defense Program Guidelines, 10 December 2004, http://www.mod.go.jp/e/d_policy/pdf/national_guideline.pdf

Table 4: **Japan Coast Guard tonnage 1988–2007**

	Patrol Craft (*junshitei*)	Patrol Vessel (*junshisen*)	Total tonnage (Patrol Vessel and Patrol Craft; *junshisentei*)	Total tonnage (*junshisentei* + hydrographic)
1988	7,000	77,000	84,000	97,000
1989	7,000	79,000	86,000	98,000
1990	7,000	79,000	86,000	98,000
1991	7,000	80,000	86,000	99,000
1992	7,000	88,000	95,000	108,000
1993	7,000	89,000	96,000	108,000
1994	8,000	89,000	97,000	110,000
1995	8,000	90,000	99,000	111,000
1996	9,000	91,000	99,000	112,000
1997	9,000	93,000	102,000	114,000
1998	9,000	96,000	104,000	117,000
1999	9,000	102,000	111,000	123,000
2000	9,000	102,000	111,000	124,000
2001	9,000	104,000	113,000	126,000
2002	10,000	104,000	114,000	127,000
2003	10,000	104,000	114,000	126,000
2004	10,000	104,000	113,000	126,000
2005	9,000	100,000	110,000	122,000
2006	9,000	105,000	115,000	127,000
2007	10,000	107,000	116,000	127,000

Source: Kaijo Hoancho Somubu Seimuka

Table 5: **JSDF recruitment 1995–2008**

Year	Category	GSDF	MSDF	ASDF	Joint Staff Council	Total for all services	Officer recruitment for all services
1995	Authorised	180,000	46,085	47,556	160	273,801	n/a
	Actual	151,555	43,748	44,574	160	239,637	n/a
	Staffing rate (%)	84.0	94.9	93.7	100.0	87.5	n/a
1996	Authorised	180,000	46,085	47,556	160	273,801	n/a
	Actual	152,515	44,135	45,883	160	242,693	n/a
	Staffing rate (%)	84.7	95.8	96.5	100.0	88.6	n/a
1997	Authorised	179,430	45,752	47,207	1,362	273,751	n/a
	Actual	152,371	43,668	45,336	1,334	242,709	n/a
	Staffing rate (%)	84.9	95.4	96.0	97.9	88.7	n/a
1998	Authorised	178,007	45,752	47,207	1,392	272,358	n/a
	Actual	151,836	43,842	45,606	1,356	242,640	n/a
	Staffing rate (%)	85.3	95.8	96.6	97.4	89.1	n/a
1999	Authorised	172,866	45,782	47,236	1,426	267,280	43,263
	Actual	145,928	43,838	45,223	1,379	236,368	42,467
	Staffing rate (%)	84.4	95.8	95.7	96.7	88.4	98.2
2000	Authorised	171,262	45,752	47,236	1,487	265,737	43,737
	Actual	148,557	42,655	44,207	1,402	236,821	42,947
	Staffing rate (%)	86.7	93.2	93.6	94.3	89.1	98.2
2001	Authorised	167,383	45,812	47,266	1,612	262,073	43,747
	Actual	148,676	44,227	45,377	1,527	239,807	43,014
	Staffing rate (%)	88.8	96.5	96.0	94.7	91.5	98.3
2002	Authorised	163,784	45,812	47,266	1,719	258,581	43,669
	Actual	148,197	44,404	45,582	1,656	239,839	42,621
	Staffing rate (%)	90.5	96.9	96.4	96.3	92.8	97.6
2003	Authorised	163,300	45,826	47,280	1,854	258,290	43,579
	Actual	148,226	44,375	45,483	1,722	239,806	42,174
	Staffing rate (%)	90.8	96.8	96.2	92.9	92.8	96.8
2004	Authorised	159,921	45,839	47,286	1,994	255,040	43,999
	Actual	146,960	44,390	45,459	1,770	238,579	41,653
	Staffing rate (%)	91.9	96.8	96.1	88.8	93.5	94.7
2005	Authorised	157,828	45,842	47,361	2,149	253,180	44,191
	Actual	147,737	44,327	45,517	1,849	239,430	41,463
	Staffing rate (%)	93.6	96.7	96.1	86.0	94.6	93.8
2006	Authorised	156,122	45,806	47,332	2,322	251,582	44,533
	Actual	148,302	44,528	45,913	2,069	240,812	41,311
	Staffing rate (%)	95.0	97.2	97.0	89.1	95.7	92.8
2007	Authorised	155,696	45,812	47,342	2,372	251,222	44,902
	Actual	148,631	44,495	45,733	2,111	240,970	41,358
	Staffing rate (%)	95.5	97.1	96.6	89.0	95.9	92.1
2008	Authorised	153,320	45,712	47,313	2,398	24,647	45,046
	Actual	138,422	44,088	45,594	2,187	230,291	41,453
	Staffing rate (%)	90.3	96.4	96.4	91.2	92.6	92.0

Source: Boeichohen/Boeishohen, *Boei Hakusho* (Tokyo: Okurasho Insatsukyoku/Zaimusho Insatsukyoku, 1997–2008)

Box 1

US–Japan SCC DPRI agreements, 2005–2006

COMMON STRATEGIC OBJECTIVES
15 FEBRUARY 2005

Common regional objectives:

- Ensure the security of Japan, strengthen peace and stability in the Asia-Pacific region, and maintain the capability to address contingencies affecting the United States and Japan.
- Support peaceful unification of the Korean Peninsula.
- Seek peaceful resolution of issues related to North Korea, including its nuclear programs, ballistic missile activities, illicit activities, and humanitarian issues such as the abduction of Japanese nationals by North Korea.
- Develop a cooperative relationship with China, welcoming the country to play a responsible and constructive role regionally as well as globally.
- Encourage the peaceful resolution of issues concerning the Taiwan Strait through dialogue.
- Encourage China to improve transparency of its military affairs.
- Encourage Russia's constructive engagement in the Asia-Pacific region.
- Fully normalize Japan–Russia relations through the resolution of the Northern Territories issue.
- Promote a peaceful, stable, and vibrant Southeast Asia.
- Welcome the development of various forms of regional cooperation, while stressing the importance of open, inclusive, and transparent regional mechanisms.
- Discourage destabilizing sales and transfers of arms and military technology.
- Maintain the security of maritime traffic.

Common global objectives:

- Promote fundamental values such as basic human rights, democracy, and the rule of law in the international community.
- Further consolidate US–Japan partnership in international peace cooperation activities and development assistance to promote peace, stability, and prosperity worldwide.
- Promote the reduction and nonproliferation of WMD and their means of delivery, including through improved reliability and effectiveness of the NPT, the International Atomic Energy Agency, and other regimes, and initiatives such as the PSI.
- Prevent and eradicate terrorism.
- Coordinate efforts to improve the effectiveness of the United Nations Security Council by making the best use of the current momentum to realize Japan's aspiration to become a permanent member.
- Maintain and enhance the stability of the global energy supply.

TRANSFORMATION AND REALIGNMENT FOR THE FUTURE
29 OCTOBER 2005

- Air defense.
- Ballistic missile defense.
- Counter-proliferation operations, such as PSI.
- Counter-terrorism.

- Minesweeping, maritime interdiction, and other operations to maintain the security of maritime traffic.
- Search and rescue operations.
- Intelligence, surveillance and reconnaissance (ISR) operations, including increasing capabilities and effectiveness of operations by UAV and maritime patrol aircraft.
- Humanitarian relief operations.
- Reconstruction assistance operations.
- Peacekeeping operations and capacity building for other nations' peacekeeping efforts.
- Protection of critical infrastructure, including US facilities and areas in Japan.
- Response to attacks by WMD, including disposal and decontamination of WMD.
- Mutual logistics support activities such as supply, maintenance, and transportation. Supply cooperation includes mutual provision of aerial and maritime refueling. Transportation cooperation includes expanding and sharing airlift and sealift, including the capability provided by high speed vessels (HSV).
- Transportation, use of facilities, medical support, and other related activities for non-combatant evacuation operations (NEO).
- Use of seaport and airport facilities, road, water space and airspace, and frequency bands.

US–JAPAN ROADMAP FOR REALIGNMENT IMPLEMENTATION 1 MAY 2006

- The relocation of the command functions of US Army I Corps from Washington State to Camp Zama near Tokyo by 2008. Japan is to complement this realignment by moving its own newly established GSDF Central Readiness Force, with rapid-reaction capabilities, to Camp Zama by 2008.
- The relocation by 2014 of the USMC Futenma air station from Futenma in Ginowan to Henoko in Nago City, involving the construction of a 'V-shaped' pair of runways; and the redeployment of the Third Marine Expeditionary Force, totalling 8,000 troops and 9,000 dependents to Guam. The move is accompanied by the relocation of USMC CH-53D helicopters to Guam, and the relocation of USMC KC-130 tankers from Okinawa to be based at Iwakuni and in Guam on a rotational basis.
- The establishment of a Bilateral Joint Operations Coordination Centre (BJOCC) at Yokota air base to collocate Japan's ASDF Command and US BMD command and control information systems, and for the US to deploy additional and complementary BMD assets around Japan, including an X-band radar system at Kashiri in Aomori Prefecture, and PAC-3 systems.
- The relocation of the US aircraft carrier wing at Atsugi air base near Tokyo to the USMC base at Iwakuni, Yamaguchi Prefecture, by 2014; and the relocation of MSDF E/O/UP-3 and U36-A to USAF Atsugi.

Sources: Ministry of Foreign Affairs Japan, 'Joint Statement US–Japan Security Consultative Committee', 19 February 2005, http://www.mofa.go.jp/region/n-america/us/security/scc/joint0502.html; Ministry of Foreign Affairs, 'Japan, Security Consultative Committee Document US–Japan Alliance: Transformation and Realignment for the Future', 29 October 2005, http://www.mofa.go.jp/region/n-america/us/security/scc/doc0510.html; Ministry of Foreign Affairs, 'United States–Japan Roadmap for Realignment Implementation', 1 May 2006, http://www.mofa.go.jp/region/n-america/us/security/scc/doc0605.html.

Chart 1

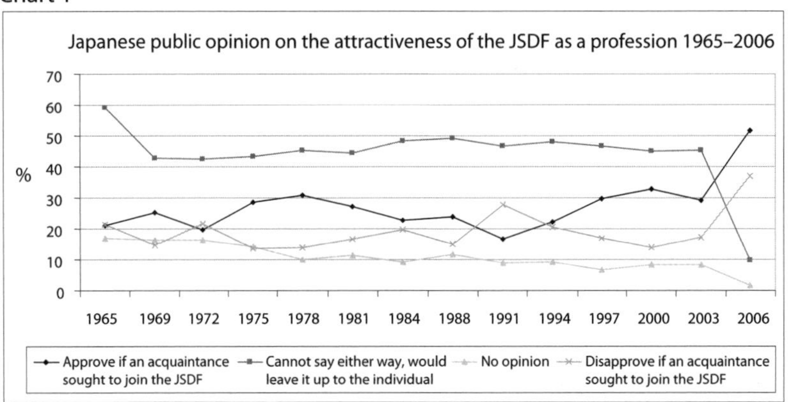

Chart 2

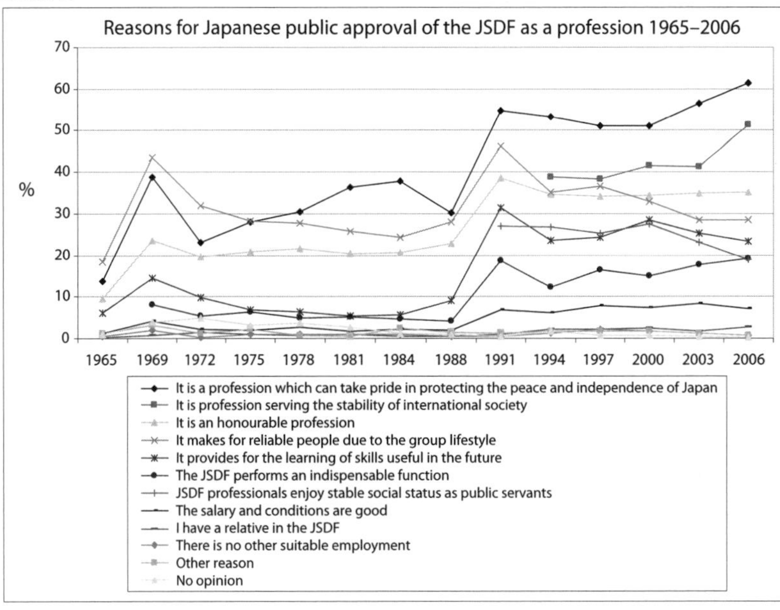

Chart 3

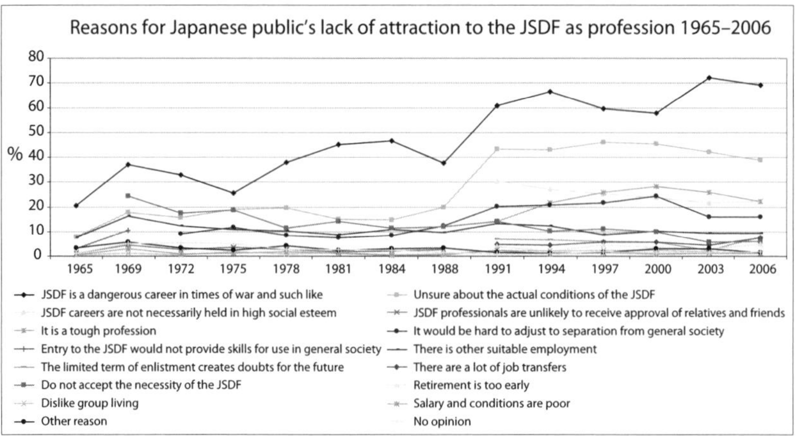
Reasons for Japanese public's lack of attraction to the JSDF as profession 1965–2006
80
70
60
50
% 40
30
20
10
0
1965 1969 1972 1975 1978 1981 1984 1988 1991 1994 1997 2000 2003 2006
JSDF is a dangerous career in times of war and such like
Unsure about the actual conditions of the JSDF
JSDF careers are not necessarily held in high social esteem
JSDF professionals are unlikely to receive approval of relatives and friends
It is a tough profession
It would be hard to adjust to separation from general society
Entry to the JSDF would not provide skills for use in general society
There is other suitable employment
The limited term of enlistment creates doubts for the future
There are a lot of job transfers
Do not accept the necessity of the JSDF
Retirement is too early
Dislike group living
Salary and conditions are poor
Other reason
No opinion

Chart 4

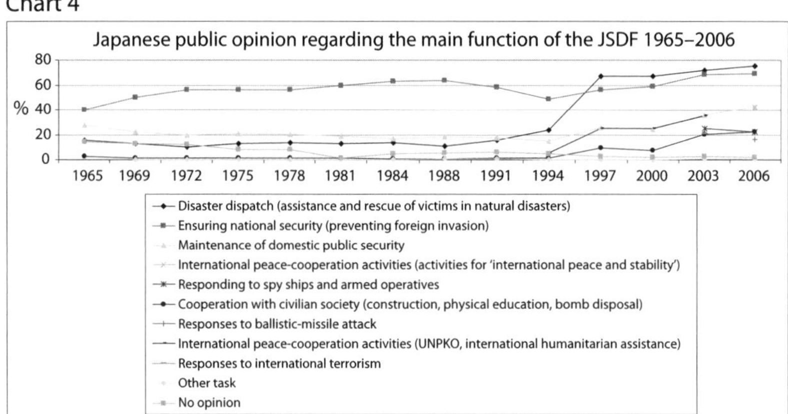
Japanese public opinion regarding the main function of the JSDF 1965–2006
80
60
% 40
20
0
1965 1969 1972 1975 1978 1981 1984 1988 1991 1994 1997 2000 2003 2006
Disaster dispatch (assistance and rescue of victims in natural disasters)
Ensuring national security (preventing foreign invasion)
Maintenance of domestic public security
International peace-cooperation activities (activities for 'international peace and stability')
Responding to spy ships and armed operatives
Cooperation with civilian society (construction, physical education, bomb disposal)
Responses to ballistic-missile attack
International peace-cooperation activities (UNPKO, international humanitarian assistance)
Responses to international terrorism
Other task
No opinion

Chart 5

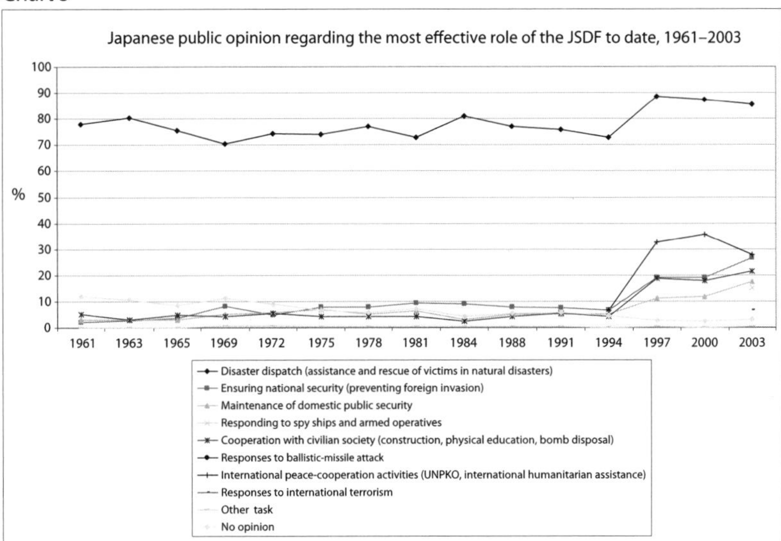

Chart 6

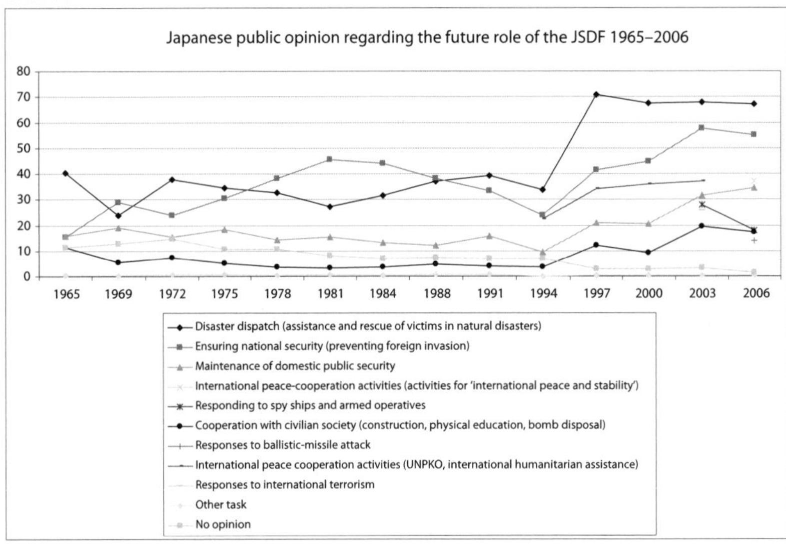

Chart 7

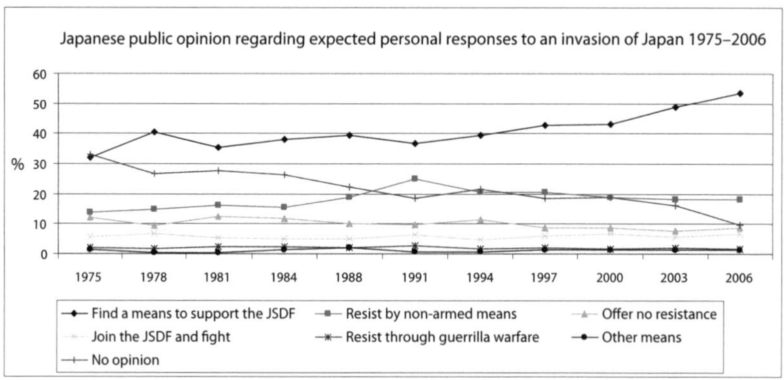

Chart 8

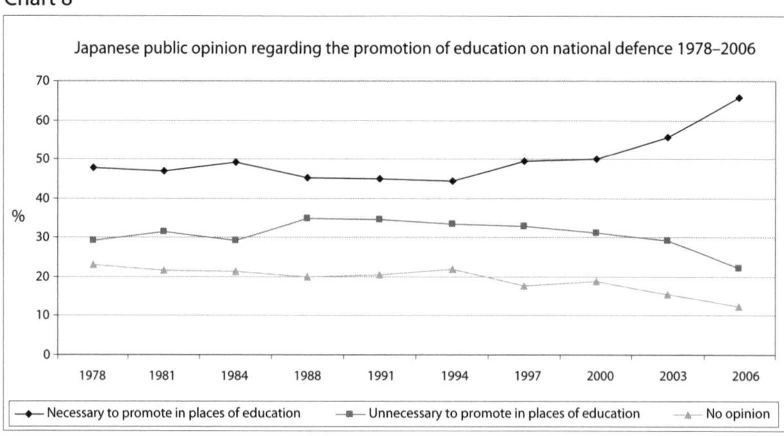

Chart 9

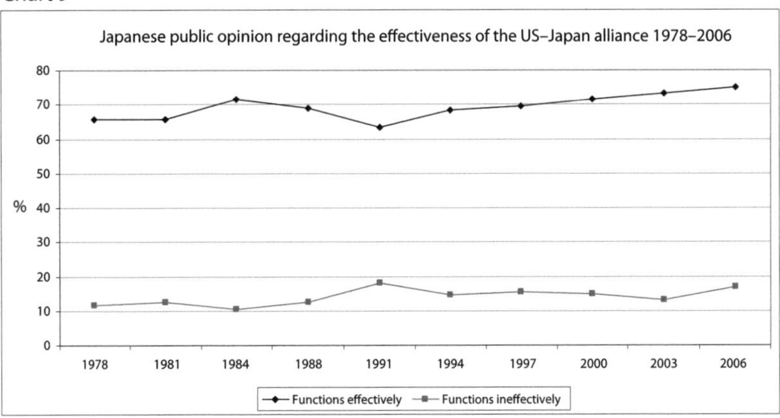

Chart 10

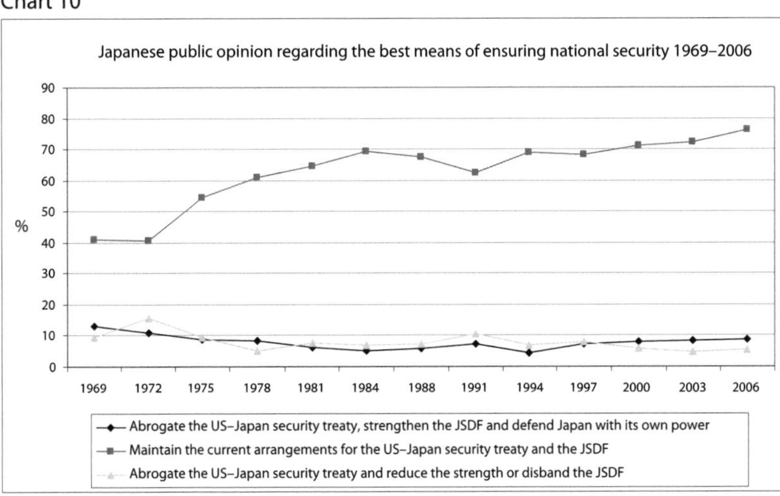

Chart 11

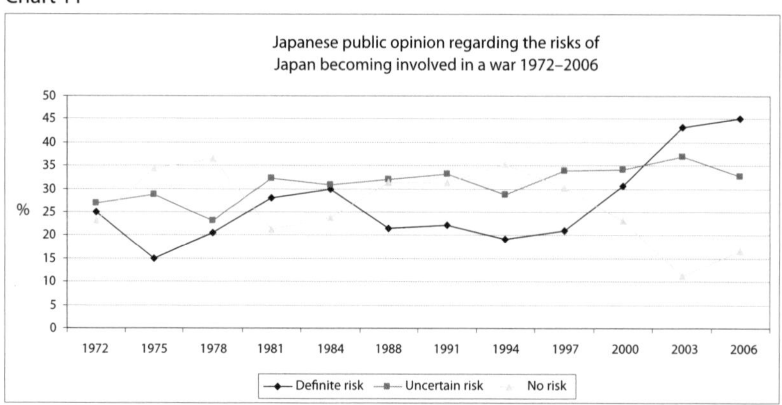

Chart 12

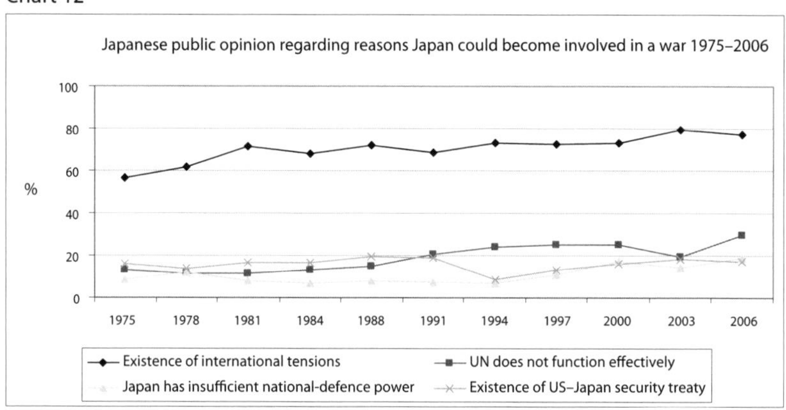

Chart 13

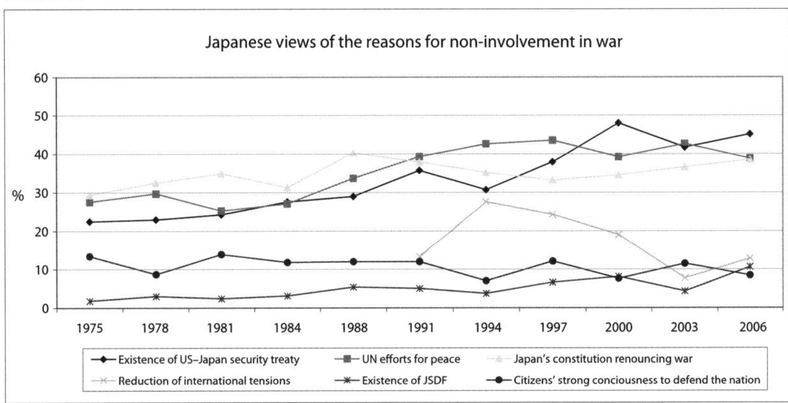

Source: Naikakufu Daijin Kanbo Seifu Kohoshitsu, *Jieitai Boei Mondai ni Kansuru Yoron Chosa*, available at http://www8.cao.go.jp/survey/index2.html

NOTES

Introduction

1 For examples arguing for a gradually more assertive Japanese military role, see Michael J. Green, *Japan's Reluctant Realism: Foreign Policy Challenges in an Era of Uncertain Power* (New York: Palgrave Macmillan, 2001); Anthony DiFilippo, *The Challenges of the US–Japan Military Arrangement: Competing Security Transitions in a Changing International Environment* (Armonk, NY: M.E. Sharpe, 2002); Gavan McCormack, 'Remilitarizing Japan', *New Left Review*, vol. 29, September–October 2004, pp. 29–44; Jennifer Lind, 'Pacifism or Passing the Buck? Testing Theories of Japanese Security Policy', *International Security*, vol. 29, no. 1, Summer 2004, pp. 92–121; Richard Tanter, 'With Eyes Wide Shut: Japan, Heisei Militarization, and the Bush Doctrine', in Mel Gurtov and Peter Van Ness (eds), *Confronting the Bush Doctrine: Critical Views from the Asia-Pacific* (London: Routledge, 2005), pp. 153–80; Christopher W. Hughes, 'Japan: Military Modernization in Search of a "Normal" Security Role', in Ashley J. Tellis and Michael Wills (eds), *Strategic Asia 2005–06: Military Modernization in an Era of Uncertainty* (Seattle, WA: National Bureau of Asian Research, 2005), pp. 105–34; Daniel M. Kliman, *Japan's Security Strategy in the Post-9/11 World: Embracing a New Realpolitik* (Westport, CT: Praeger/CSIS, 2006); Kenneth B. Pyle, *Japan Rising: The Resurgence of Japanese Power and Purpose* (New York: Public Affairs Books, 2007); Richard J. Samuels, *Securing Japan: Tokyo's Grand Strategy and the Future of East Asia* (Ithaca, NY: Cornell University Press, 2007).

2 For examples arguing for continued strong Japanese resistance to further remilitarisation post-11 September, see Thomas U. Berger, 'Japan's International Relations: The Political and Security Dimensions', in Samuel S. Kim (ed.), *The International Relations of Northeast Asia* (Lanham, MD: Rowman Littlefield and Publishers, 2004), pp. 135–69; H. Richard Friman, Peter J. Katzenstein, David Leheny and Nobuo Okawara, 'Immovable Object? Japan's Security Policy in East Asia', in Peter J. Katzenstein and Takashi Shiraishi, *Beyond Japan: The Dynamics of East Asian Regionalism* (Ithaca, NY: Cornell

University Press, 2006), pp. 85–107; Paul Midford, 'Japanese Mass Opinion Toward the War on Terrorism', in Robert D. Eldridge and Paul Midford (eds), *Japanese Public Opinion and the War on Terrorism* (New York: Palgrave Macmillan, 2008), pp. 11–42; Andrew L. Oros, *Normalizing Japan: Politics, Identity and the Evolution of Security Practice* (Stanford, CA: Stanford University Press, 2008); Yasuo Takao, *Is Japan Really Remilitarising? The Politics of Norm Formation and Change* (Clayton: Monash University Press, 2008).

3 For examples arguing for Japan's long-term remilitarisation post-Koizumi, see Gavan McCormack, *Client State: Japan in the American Embrace* (London: Verso, 2007); Testuo Maeda, *Jieitai: Henyo no Yukie* (Tokyo: Iwanami Shinsho, 2007); Christopher W. Hughes and Ellis S. Krauss, 'Japan's New Security Agenda', *Survival*, vol. 49, no. 2, Spring 2007, pp. 157–76.

4 Christopher W. Hughes, *Japan's Reemergence as a 'Normal' Military Power*, Adelphi Paper 368/9 (Oxford: OUP for the IISS, 2004).

5 The literature on militarisation and militarism is well established in social science, drawing on rich and diverse insights from political science, sociology, social anthropology, economics and international relations. For overall statements of the classical indicators of remilitarisation, see Alfred Vagts, *A History of Militarism* (Westport, CT: Greenwood Press, 1959); Kjell Skjelsbaek, 'Militarism, Its Dimensions and Corollaries: An Attempt at Conceptual Clarification', *Journal of Peace Research*, vol. 16, no. 3, 1979, pp. 213–29; Volker R. Berghahn, *Militarism: The History of an International Debate, 1861–1979* (Leamington Spa: Berg Publishers, 1981); Martin Shaw, *Post-Military Society: Militarism, Demilitarization and War at the End of the Twentieth Century* (Cambridge: Polity Press, 1991). For debates on civil–military relations and the indicators of remilitarisation, see Harold D. Lasswell, 'The Garrison State', *American Journal of Sociology*, vol. 46, no. 4, 1941, pp. 455–68; Samuel P. Huntington, *The Soldier and the State: The Theory and Politics of Civil–Military Relations* (Cambridge, MA: Belknap Press, 1964); Morris Janowitz, *The Professional Soldier: A Social and Political Portrait* (New York: The Free Press, 1971); Samuel E. Finer, *The Man on Horseback: The Role of the Military in Politics*, 2nd edition (Boulder, CO: Westview Press, 1988). For the concept of the military-industrial complex, see Rosa Luxemburg, *The Accumulation of Capital* (London: Routledge, 1961); Joseph Schumpeter, *Sociology of Imperialism* (New York: Meridian, 1955); C. Wright Mills, *The Power Elite* (Oxford: Oxford University Press, 1956); Jerome Slater and Terry Nardin, 'The Concept of a Military-Industrial Complex', in Steven Rosen (ed.), *Testing the Theory of the Military-Industrial Complex* (Lexington, MA: Lexington Books, 1973), pp. 27–60; Mary Kaldor, *The Baroque Arsenal* (London: Andrei Deutsch, 1982); Dan Smith and Ron Smith, *The Economics of Militarism* (London: Pluto Press, 1982); Keith Krause, *Arms and the State: Patterns of Military Production and Trade* (Cambridge: Cambridge University Press, 1992).

6 For a history of Japan's self-declared constraints on remilitarisation, see Glenn D. Hook, *Demilitarization and Remilitarization in Contemporary Japan* (London: Routledge, 1996).

Chapter One

1 Ian Gow, 'Civilian Control of the Military in Post-war Japan', in Ron Matthews and Keisuke Matsuyama (eds), *Japan's Military Renaissance?* (Basingstoke: Macmillan, 1993); Yale Candee Maxon, *Control of Japanese Foreign Policy: A Study in Civil–Military Rivalry* (Berkeley, CA: University of California Press, 1957), pp. 1–34 and 51–53; Richard J. Samuels, *Rich Nation, Strong Army: National Security and the Technological Transformation of Japan* (Ithaca, NY: Cornell University Press, 1994), pp. 79–107; Isamu Hatano, *Kindai Nihon no Gunsangaku Fukugotai: Kaigun, Jukogyo, Daigaku* (Tokyo: Sobunsha, 2005).

2 Glenn D. Hook, 'The Erosion of Anti-Militaristic Principles in Contemporary Japan', *Journal of Peace Research*, vol. 25, no. 4, 1988, pp. 381–2.

3 John Dower, *Embracing Defeat: Japan in the Aftermath of World War II* (London: Penguin Books, 1999), pp. 73–80 and 346–404.

4 Christopher W. Hughes, 'Why Japan Could Revise Its Constitution and What It Would Mean for Japanese Security Policy', *Orbis*, vol. 50, no. 4, Autumn 2006, p. 728.

5 Christopher W. Hughes and Akiko Fukushima, 'Japan–US Security Relations: Toward "Bilateralism-Plus"?', in Ellis. S. Krauss and T.J. Pempel (eds), *Beyond Bilateralism: The US–Japan Relationship in the New Asia-Pacific* (Stanford, CA: Stanford University Press, 2004), pp. 60–1.

6 Since 1978, Japan has loosely defined an offensive carrier as the types possessed by the US, presumably those with fixed-wing aircraft, and defensive carriers as those carrying helicopters for anti-submarine warfare. Yoshimitsu Nishikawa, *Nihon Anzen Hosho Seisaku* (Tokyo: Shoyo Shobo, 2008), pp. 163–4. Japan's full prohibition on power-projection capabilities was outlined by Japan Defense Agency (JDA) Director General Tsutomu Kawara in National Diet House of Councillors Budget Committee interpellations on 6 April 1988. See Asagumo Shimbunsha, *Boei Handobukku 2007* (Tokyo: Asagumo Shimbunsha 2007), pp. 607–8.

7 For the background to Japan's arms-export bans, see Oros, *Normalizing Japan*, pp. 94–109.

8 Michael J. Green, *Arming Japan: Defense Production, Alliance Politics, and the Postwar Search for Autonomy* (New York: Columbia University Press, 1995), pp. 86–124; Glenn D. Hook, *Demilitarization and Remilitarization in Contemporary Japan* (London: Routledge, 1996), pp. 45–99.

9 For examples of the view that the glass of Japanese of remilitarisation was half-empty rather than half-full, see Thomas U. Berger, 'From Sword to Chrysanthemum: Japan's Culture of Anti-Militarism', *International Security*, vol. 17, no. 4, Spring 1993, pp. 119–50; Peter J. Katzenstein and Nobuo Okawara, 'Japan's National Security: Structures, Norms, and Policies', *ibid.*, pp. 84–118.

10 Christopher W. Hughes, '"Super-Sizing" the DPRK Threat: Japan's Evolving Military Posture and North Korea', *Asian Survey*, vol. 49, no. 2, March–April 2009.

11 Boeisho, 'Kokusai Gunji Josei: Wagakuni Shuhen Josei o Chushin ni, Anzen Hosho to Boeiryoku ni Kansuru', Kondankai Dai2kai Gijishidai, January 2009, http://

www.kantei.go.jp/jp/singi/ampoboueiz/dai2/siryou2.pdf, p. 14. For descriptions of the difficulties of estimating China's real level of defence expenditure, see International Institute for Strategic Studies, *The Military Balance 2009* (London: Routledge, 2009), pp. 375–6.

12 'Missairu Yogekiami ni Shingata Reda Chokyoridan, Boeisho Hoshin', *Yomiuri Shimbun*, 27 January 2008, http://www.yomiuri.co.jp/politics/news/20080127-OYT1T00018.htm.

13 Boeishohen, *Boei Hakusho 2008* (Tokyo: Zaimusho Insatsukyoku, 2008), pp. 50–1; Boeisho Boeikenkyusho, *Higashi Ajia Senryku Gaikan 2008* (Tokyo: The Japan Times, 2008), pp. 16–33. For the background on China's anti-satellite test and its growing military capabilities in space, see Tai Ming Cheung, *Fortifying China: The Struggle To Build a Modern Defense Economy* (Ithaca, NY: Cornell University Press, 2009), pp. 249–55.

14 Boeishohen, *Boei Hakusho 2008*, p. 66.

15 US Department of Defense, *Quadrennial Defense Review Report 2001* (Washington DC: US Government Printing Office (USGPO), 30 September 2001), http://www.defenselink.mil/pubs/pdfs/qdr2001.pdf, pp. 25–7; The White House, *The National Security Strategy of The United States of America* (Washington DC: USGPO, September 2002), pp. 22–4; US Department of Defense, *The National Defense Strategy of The United States of America* (Washington DC: USGPO, March 2005), pp. 12, 15 and 17; US Department of Defense, *Quadrennial Defense Review Report 2006* (Washington DC: USGPO, 6 February 2006), p. 18; Yoko Iwama, 'The New Shape of the US Alliance System', *Gaiko Forum*, Spring 2004, pp. 28–9.

Chapter Two

1 JDA, *National Defense Program Guidelines, FY 2005–*, http://www.jda.go.jp, pp. 2–3.

2 *Ibid.*, p. 9.

3 Boeishohen, *Boei Hakusho 2008* (Tokyo: Zaimusho Insatsukyoku, 2008), p. 333.

4 Asagumo Shimbunsha, *Boei Handobukku 1997* (Tokyo: Asagumo Shimbunsha, 1997), pp. 268–70; Asagumo Shimbunsha, *Boei Handobukku 1998* (Tokyo: Asagumo Shimbunsha, 1998), pp. 268–70; Asagumo Shimbunsha, *Boei Handobukku 2007* (Tokyo: Asagumo Shimbunsha, 2007), p. 336; Boeishohen, *Boei Hakusho 2008* (Tokyo: Zaimusho Insatsukyoku, 2008), p. 334

5 Boeisho, *Waga Kuni no Boei to Yosan, Heisei 21nendo Gaisan Yokyu no Gaiyo* (Tokyo: Boeisho, 2008), http://www.mod.go.jp/j/library/archives/yosan/2009/yosan.pdf, p. 28; Boeisho, *Waga Kuni no Boei to Yosan, Heisei 21nendo Yosan no Gaiyo* (Tokyo: Boeisho, 2008), http://www.mod.go.jp/j/library/archives/yosan/2009/yosan.pdf, p. 28. In response to rising fuel costs, in 2008 MSDF ships ran at reduced speeds to conserve fuel, and the ASDF likewise reduced low-flying exercises. However, problems with fuel costs did not prevent the GSDF from holding its largest exercise since 1994 for territorial defence, involving over 3,000

personnel. The exercise took place in October 2008 in Hokkaido. See 'Genyu de Kaiji Enshu ga Chushi no Kanosei, Kuji wa Teikuhiko o Sakugen', *Yomiuri Shimbum*, 26 August 2008, http://www.yomiuri.co.jo/national/news/20080826-OYT1T00443.htm; 'GSDF Stages Huge Defense Drill', *Japan Times Online*, 28 October 2008, http://www.japantimes.co.jp/print/20081028a5.html.

6 Kent E. Calder, *Crisis and Compensation: Public Policy and Political Stability in Japan* (Princeton, NJ: Princeton University Press, 1988), pp. 437–8.

7 'Beitaishi ga Koen, Nihon no Boeihi "Zogaku Subeki"', *Yomiuri Shimbun*, 20 May 2008, http://www.yomiuri.co.jo/national/news/20080520-OYT1T00608.htm.

8 For an example of Japan comparing its defence expenditure with NATO's, see Boeishohen, *Boei Hakusho 2008* (Tokyo: Zaimusho Insatsukyoku, 2008), p. 122. For Japan's methodology for calculating defence expenditures without including the JCG, see Chuma Kiyofuku, *Gunjihi o Yomu, Iwanami Bukuretto No. 68* (Tokyo: Iwanami Shoten, 1986), pp. 42–49.

9 Kaijo Hoancho, *Kaijo Hoanchoho*, 1948, http://law.e-gov.go.jp/htmldata/S23/S23HO028.html.

10 Naigai Shuppanhen, *Boeicho Kankei Horeishu* (Tokyo: Naigai Shuppan, 2005), p. 71; The JCG is defined as a paramilitary force in *The Military Balance*. See IISS, *The Military Balance 2009*, p. 394.

11 David Leheny, *Think Global, Fear Local: Sex, Violence and Anxiety in Contemporary Japan* (Ithaca, NY: Cornell University Press, 2006), pp. 157–69; Richard J. Samuels, *Securing Japan: Tokyo's Grand Strategy and the Future of East Asia* (Ithaca, NY: Cornell University Press, 2007), pp. 78–9; Richard J. Samuels, '"New Fighting Power!" Japan's Growing Maritime Capabilities and East Asian Security', *International Security*, vol. 32, no. 3, Winter 2007–08, pp. 84–112.

12 Maeda Testuo, *Jieitai: Henyo no Yukie* (Tokyo: Iwanami Shinsho, 2007), pp. 144–5.

13 Harrison M. Holland, *Managing Defense: Japan's Dilemma* (New York: University Press of America, 1988), pp. 34–5; Michael E. Chinworth, *Inside Japan's Defense: Technology, Economics and Strategy* (Washington DC: Brassey's US, 1992), p. 63; Masako Ikegami-Andersson, 'Arms Procurement Decision Making: Japan', in Ravinder Pal Singh (ed.), *Arms Procurement Decision Making Volume I: China, India, Israel, Japan, South Korea and Thailand* (Oxford: OUP for SIPRI, 1998).

14 Kaijo Hoancho Somubu Seimuka 2007, figures provided via National Diet Library, 2007; IISS, *The Military Balance 2009*, p. 394.

15 'Kenkyu Chakushu Miokuri: Choshatei Yudodan', *Asahi Shimbun*, 8 December 2004, p. 3.

16 'Sentoheli Appachi Chotatsu Chushi, Ichiki 2000kuen ni Neagari de', *Yomiuri Shimbun*, 23 August 2008, http://www.yomiuri.co.jp/politics/news/20080823-OYT1T00413.htm.

17 'F15 Kaisu 9470kuen, FX Sentei Nanko Boeisho Gaisan Yokyu', *Asahi Shimbun*, 27 August 2008, http://www.asahi.com/politics/update/0827/TKY200808270036.html; Boeisho, *Waga Kuni no Boei to Yosan, Heisei 21nendo Yosan no Gaiyo*, pp. 21–2.

18 'Kimaranu Jiki Sentoki: Boeisho Chugoku wa Gunji Zokyo Bokuryoku ni Kennen', *Nihon Keizai Shimbun*, 26 August 2008, p. 2.

[19] 'Beitaishi ga Koen, Nihon no Boeihi "Zogaku Subeki"', *Yomiuri Shimbun*, 20 May 2008, http://www.yomiuri.co.jo/national/news/20080520-OYT1T00608.htm.

[20] Boeisho, *Waga Kuni no Boei to Yosan, Heisei 21nendo Yosan no Gaiyo*, p. 23.

[21] Richard L. Armitage and Joseph S. Nye, *The US-Japan Alliance: Getting Asia Right Through 2020* (Washington DC: CSIS, February 2007), http://www.csis.org/media/csis/pubs/070216_asia2020.pdf2020, p. 28.

[22] Alexander Neill, Jonathan Eyal and John Hemmings (eds), *Delivering Defence Industrial Change* (London: Royal United Services Institute, 2008), http://www.rusi.org/downloads/assets/JapanEnglish.pdf, p. 61.

[23] Christopher Bolkcom and Emma Chanlett-Avery, *Potential F-22 Raptor Export to Japan, CRS Report for Congress* (Washington DC: Congressional Research Service, 2 July 2007), p. 5; 'Visiting F-22s Waging a War with the Bean Counters', *Japan Times Online*, 23 February 2009, http://search.japntimes.co.jp/print/nn20090223a9.html.

[24] 'Boei Yosan no Gaisan Yokyu, Nenryo Kosho de Sogaku 4cho 8448okuen', *Yomiuri Shimbun*, 27 August 2008, http://www.yomiuri.co.jp/politics/news/20080827-OYT1T00401.htm.

[25] 'Heri Kubo "Hygua" Haibi Yokosuka ni Atarashii Goeikan', *Asahi Shimbun*, 19 March 2009, http://www.asahi.com/national/update/0318/TKY200903180279.html.

[26] Ebata Kensuke, *Nihon no Gunji Shisutemu: Jieitai Sobi no Mondaiten* (Tokyo: Kodansha, 2004), pp. 227–8.

[27] 'MSDF's SM-3 Test Fails To Shoot Down Missile', *Japan Times Online*, 21 November 2008, http://searchjapantimes.co.jp/print/nn20081121a3.html; 'Despite Failure, Missile Defense System OK'd', *ibid.*, 17 December 2008, http://searchjapantimes.co.jp/print/nn20081217a3.html.

[28] 'Tokyo-area Gets Last PAC-3 Battery', *ibid.*, 30 March 2008, http://searchjapantimes.co.jp/print/nn20080330a9.html.

[29] 'Yogeki Missairu, Yoyogi Koen Nado de Tenkai Kento Kugatsu ni mo Kunren', *Asahi Shimbun*, 31 August 2007, http://www.asahi.com/politics/update/0830/TKY200708300385.html.

[30] 'MSDF Fails To Intercept Missile in Test', *Daily Yomiuri Online*, 21 November 2008, http://www.yomiuri.co.jp/dy/world/20081121TDY01303.htm.

[31] 'Missile Attack Alarm Falsely Tripped', *Japan Times Online*, 14 August 2008, http://search.japantimes.co.jp/print/nn20080815a8.html.

[32] Aoki Setsuko, *Nihon no Uchu Senryaku* (Tokyo: Keio Gijuku Daigaku Shuppan, 2006), pp. 177–80; Oros, *Normalizing Japan*, p. 137.

[33] For a detailed account of Japan's introduction of the IGSs, see Sunohara Tsuyoshi, *Tanjo Kokusan Supai Eisei: Dokuji Joho to Nichibei Domei* (Tokyo: Nihon Keizai Shimbunsha, 2005).

[34] Pat Norris, *Spies in the Sky: Surveillance Satellites in War and Peace* (New York: Springer, 2008), p. 180.

[35] Suzuki Kazuto, 'Space: Japan's New Security Agenda', *RIPS Policy Perspectives*, 5 October 2007, http://www.rips.or.jp/English/publications/rips_pp_5.html.

[36] Kokkai Shugiin, *Uchu Kihon Hoan*, May 2008, http://www.shugiin.go.jp/index.nsf/html/index_gian.htm.

[37] Shusho Kantei, *Uchu Kaihatsu Senryaku Semonin Chosakai Koseiin*, August 2008,

http://www.kantei.go.jp/jp/singi/utyuu/pdf/1.pdf.

38 Japan Ministry of Defense, *Space Related Defence Policies and Future Topics for Consideration*, November 2008, http://www.mod.go.jp/e/d_policy/pdf/space2008.pdf, p. 4.

39 'Govt May Propose Missile Defense Satellite', *Yomiuri Shimbun*, 5 November 2008, http://www.yomiuri.co.jp/dy/national/20081105TDY020307.htm.

40 Boeisho Uchu Kaihatsu Riyo Iinkai, *Uchu Kaihatsu Riyo ni Kansuru Kihon Hoshin ni Tsuite*, 15 January 2009, http://www.mod.go.jp/j/info/uchuukaihatsu/pdf/kihonhoushin.pdf, pp. 4, 6.

41 'Uchu no Boei Riyo Kaikin, Gijutsu Kenkyu no Keikakushitsu Shinsetsu e, Boeisho', *Yomiuri Shimbun*, 28 August 2008, http://www.yomiuri.co.jp/politics/news/20080828-OYT1T00100.htm.

42 Samuels, '"New Fighting Power!"', p. 99.

43 Christopher W. Hughes, *Japan's Security Agenda: Military, Economic and Environmental Dimensions* (Boulder: CO, Lynne Rienner, 2004), pp. 222–6.

44 'Boei Taiko Kaitei Honkaku Giron e: Chucho Kokusai Koken ni Juten', *Nihon Keizai Shimbun*, 9 January 2009, p. 2; Kaneko Masafumi, 'Boei Taiko o Do Minaosu ka', *PHP Policy Review*, vol. 2, no. 11, 10 December 2008, p. 7

Chapter Three

1 Tsuneo Watanabe, 'The Bankruptcy of Civil–Military Relations in Japan', *NIRA Review*, Summer 1996, http://www.nira.or.jp/past/publ/review/96summer/watanabe.html.

2 Richard J. Samuels, *Politics, Security, and Japan's Cabinet Legislation Bureau: Who Elected These Guys Anyway?*, *JPRI Working Paper*, no. 99, March 2004, http://www.jpri.org/publications/workingpapers/wp99.html.

3 Koketsu Atsushi, *Bumin Tosei: Jieitai wa Doko Iku Ka* (Tokyo: Iwanami Shoten, 2005), p. 6.

4 The *Mitsuya Kenkyu* or *Three Arrows Study* incident was exposed by SDPJ member Haruo Okada on 10 February 1965, when he charged that the JSDF under its 1963 General Defense Plan of Operation had been planning to establish an authoritarian government in Japan in the event of a crisis on the Korean Peninsula. Okada also claimed that the *Mitsuya Kenkyu* contained the following items: Japan would be an integral part of US strategy in the Far East and serve as the base for US operations; the JSDF would train jointly with US, Taiwanese and South Korean troops; in another Korean crisis precipitated by a North Korean and Chinese invasion of South Korea, the JSDF would fulfill defensive assignments, including the blockade of the eastern coast of China, as well as acting as a reserve force in Japan, Korea and Manchuria; and that, during a period of emergency, Japan as a whole would be mobilised with necessary agencies to control and regulate services previously managed by civilian bodies. Prime Minister Eisaku Sato at first denied the existence of the General Defense Plan of Operation, but

later acknowledged that it was real, though he defended it on the grounds that it was merely a theoretical study by the JSDF and not a national defence plan. For more details see Christopher W. Hughes, *Japan's Economic Power and Security: Japan and North Korea* (London: Routledge, 1999), p. 58. For the Kurisu incident, see Katsuya Hirose, *Kanryo to Gunjin: Bunmin Tosei no Genkai* (Tokyo: Iwanami Shoten, 1989); Atsushi Koketsu, *Bumin Tosei: Jieitai wa Doko Iku Ka* (Tokyo: Iwanami Shoten, 2005), p. 45.

5 Shigenobu Tamura, *Boeisho Tanjo: Sono Igi to Rekishi* (Tokyo: Naigai Shuppan, 2007), pp. 53–66.

6 Koketsu, *Bumin Tosei: Jieitai wa Doko Iku Ka*, pp. 47–8; Eiichi Katahara, 'Japan: From Containment to Normalization', in Muthiah Alagappa (ed.), *Coercion and Governance: The Declining Political Role of the Military in Asia* (Stanford, CA: Stanford University Press, 2001), p. 82; Funabashi Yoichi, *Domei Hyoryu* (Tokyo: Iwanami Shoten, 1997), pp. 128–33.

7 Koketsu, *Bumin Tosei: Jieitai wa Doko Iku Ka*, pp. 47–8, 55; 'Gear Shift on Constitutional Change', *Japan Times Online*, 24 December 2004, http://search.japantimes.co.jp/cgi-bin/ed20041224a5.html.

8 Boeisho, *Boeisho Secchiho*, 2007, http://law.e-gov.go.jp/htmldata/S29/S29HO164.html.

9 The wording of the section up until 2002 had read: 'At the JDA, the Director General administers and controls the JSDF. The Director General is assisted in policy and planning by the Senior Vice-Minister for Defense and two Parliamentary Secretaries for Defense. In addition, the Administrative Vice-Minister supports the Director General and oversees the administration, and the Defense Counsellors assist the Director General regarding the basic direction of policy' (author's translation). The new wording of this section deleted the second sentence and the reference to the role of the administrative vice-minister and defense counsellors in civilian control altogether. For a comparison of the two texts, see Boeichohen, *Boei Hakusho 2002* (Tokyo: Zaimusho Insatsukyoku, 2002), p. 88; Boeichohen, *Boei Hakusho 2003* (Tokyo: Zaimusho Insatsukyoku, 2003), p. 90.

10 Koketsu, *Bumin Tosei: Jieitai wa Doko Iku Ka*, pp. 2–3.

11 'Admiral Proposes SDF Less Run by Civilians', *Japan Times Online*, 3 July 2004, http://search.japantimes.co.jp/cgi-bin/nn20040703a1.html.

12 Defense Policy Studies Subcommittee, National Defense Division, Policy Research Council, Liberal Democratic Party, *Recommendations on Japan's New Defense Policy: Toward a Safer and More Secure Japan in the World*, 30 March 2003, http://www.jimin.jp/jimin/main/seisaku.html.

13 'Defense Agency To Retain Civilian Buffer Around Chief', *Japan Times Online*, 28 December 2004, http://search.japantimes.co.jp/cgi-bin/nn20041228a5.html; Boeichohen, *Boei Hakusho 2007* (Tokyo: Zaimusho Insatsukyoku, 2007), p. 164.

14 Boeichohen, *Boei Hakusho 2003*, pp. 305–6.

15 Teruaki Koide, 'Sengo no Nihon no Seigun Kamkei: Bunkan Yui Seido o Chushin ni', *Kokusai Seiji*, no. 154, December 2008, p. 88.

16 Boeicho, *Boeicho Secchiho Nado o Ichibu o Kaisei Suru Horitsuan Kankei Shiryo* (Tokyo: Boeicho, 2005), http://law.e-

gov.go.jp/htmldata/S29/S29HO164.html.

17 'Boei Naikyoku mo Kyuyuryo Minshu "Naikyoku Inpei" Tsuikyu', *Asahi Shimbun*, 27 October 2007, http://www.asahi.com/politics/update/1026/TKY200710260363.html.

18 'Seifukugumi no Kokkai Toben Kento Bunmin Tosei Meguri Giron', *ibid.*, 29 October 2007, http://www.asahi.com/politics/update/1026/TKY200710260364.html.

19 Shigeru Ishiba, 'Ishiba Boeisho no Soshiki no Arikata ni Tsuite no Iken Gaiyo', 13 February 2008, http://www.kantei.go.jp/jp/singi/bouei/dai5/pdf/siryou3.pdf.

20 'Boeisho Saihen Koso de Hamon Sebirugumi Seifukugumi no Togo Hakaru Daijin', *Asahi Shimbun*, 13 February 2008, http://www.asahi.com/politics/update/0212/TKY200802120290.html.

21 'Boeisho ni Saiko Ishi Kettei Kikan, Sebirogumi Seifukugumi ga Ittai de Kyogi', *Yomiuri Shimbun*, 25 April 2008, http://www.yomiuri.co.jp/politics/news/20080425-OYT1T00009.htm.

22 Jiyu Minshuto Seimu Chosakai Boeisho Kaikaku Shoiinkai, *Teigen: Boeisho Kaikaku*, 24 April 2008, http://www.jimin.jp/jimin/seisaku/2008/pdf/seisaku-008.pdf.

23 Boeisho Kaikaku Kaigi, *Hokokusho: Fuyoji no Bunseki to Kaikaku Hokosei*, 15 July 2008, http://www.kantei.go.jp/jp/singi/bouei/dai11/pdf/siryou.pdf, p. 40.

24 *Ibid.*, pp. 41–5.

25 'Boeisho Saisei: Chukan Shireibu Nado Shoten ni', *Nihon Keizai Shimbun*, 29 July 2008, p. 2.

26 Minister's Secretariat, Ministry of Defense, Policy Planning and Evaluation Division, 'Reform of the Ministry of Defense', January 2009, http://www.mod.go.jp/e/d_policy/reform/pdf/reform200902.pdf, p. 2.

27 Boeisho, *22nen ni Okeru Boeisho Soshiki Kaikaku ni Kansuru Kihon Kangaekata*, 22 December 2008, http://www.mod.go.jp/j/news/kaikaku/20081222b.pdf.

28 Toshio Tamogami, 'Was Japan an Aggressor Nation?', May 2008, http://www.apa.co.jp/book_report/images/2008jyusyou_saiyuusyu_english.pdf.

29 Ministry of Foreign Affairs Japan, 'Statement by Prime Minister Tomiichi Murayama on the Occasion of the 50th Anniversary of the War's End, 15 August 1995', http://www.mofa.go.jp/announce/press/pm/murayama/9508.html.

30 'Sengo Kyoiku de Shiki Teika: Hanron Fusatsu Nara Kitachosen', *Mainichi Shimbun*, 4 November 2008, p. 2.

31 'Tamogami Behind 78 Other ASDF Essay Entries', *Japan Times Online*, 7 November 2008, http://www.japantimes.co.jp/print/nn20081107a1.html; 'Essay Judges Defend Tamogami', *ibid.*, 9 December 2008, http://www.japantimes.co.jp/print/nn20081209a3.html.

32 'Masuda Defends "Hawkish" Classes', *ibid.*, 21 November 2008, http://www.japantimes.co.jp/print/nn20081121a4.html.

33 'Kujishi de mo "Shinryaku Uso"', *Asahi Shimbun*, 3 November 2008, p. 31.

34 'Kubakucho Kaishoku, Jusho Happyo Tojitsu ni Shusho ga Shiji', *Yomiuri Shimbun*, 11 November 2008, http://www.yomiuri.co.jp/politics/news/20081111-OYT1T0014.htm.

36 *Kokkai Sangiin Kaigiroku Gaiko Boei Iinkai*, 6go, 11 November 2008, p. 70, available at http://kokkai.ndl.go.jp; 'Tamogami Maekubakucho ga Shiji Hitei "Sureba 1000nin Toko"', *Asahi Shimbun*, 11 November 2008, http://

www.asahi.com/politics/update/1111/TKY200811110133.html.

36 'Maekubakucho, Shusho "Kiwamete Futekisetsu" Sanin Gaiko Boei I', *ibid.*, http://www.asahi.com/politics/update/1113/TKY200811130125.html.

37 'SDF's Rise in '90s Behind Tamogami's Challenge', *Japan Times*, 28 November 2008, http://www.japantimes.co.jo/print/nn20081128f1.html.

38 Soichiro Tahara, 'The Tamogami Debacle: Dismissal of a Japanese General and the Danger of Indignation', *Japan Focus*, 21 November 2008, http://www.japanfocus.org/_Tahara_Soichiro__H_Bix/2958.

39 Boeisho Kaikaku Kaigi, *12kai Giji Yoshi*, 25 December 2008, http://www.kantei.go.jp/jp/singi/bouei/dai12/pdf/12gijiyousi.pdf, p. 2.

Chapter Four

1 For US–Japan defence-production linkages, see Samuels, *Rich Nation, Strong Army*; Green, *Arming Japan*.

2 Chinworth, *Inside Japan's Defense*.

3 Samuels, *Rich Nation, Strong Army*, pp. 154–97.

4 Asagumo Shimbunsha, *Boei Handobukku 2008* (Tokyo: Asagumo Shimbunsha, 2008), p. 360.

5 *Ibid.*, p. 360.

6 Boei Kankokai Henshubu, *Boei Nenkan 2008* (Tokyo: Kankokai Henshubu, 2008), pp. 506–9.

7 '2007 Top 100', *Defense News*, http://www.defensenews.com/static/features/top100/charts/rank_2007.php?c=FEA&s=T1C.

8 Chinworth, *Inside Japan's Defense*, pp. 21–6; Green, *Arming Japan*, p. 122; Ikegami-Andersson, 'Arms Procurement Decision Making: Japan', p. 168; Yukari Kubota, 'Nihon no Boei Sangyo no Tokushitsu', *Kokusai Seiji*, vol. 131, November 2002, pp. 114–15; Boei Kankokai Henshubu, *Boei Nenkan 2008* (Tokyo: Kankokai Henshubu, 2008), p. 510.

9 'Itochu Kogaisha mo Moriya Hikoku o Gorufu Settai Keijunikai', *Asahi Shimbun*, 18 February 2008, http://www.asahi.com/special/071029/TKY200802180474.html.

10 'Shikin Ryunyu "Nai" Kyuma-shi Seikai Kanyo o Hitei', *ibid.*, 25 July 2008, p. 4. For an insider's account of Kyuma's alleged implication in corruption associated with Miyazaki, see Naoki Akiyama, *Boei Gikoku* (Tokyo: Kodansha, 2008), pp. 58–66. For more on defence-related scandals, see Nobumasa Ota, *Jitsumei Kokuhatsu Boeisho* (Tokyo: Kinobi, 2008).

11 Boeisho, *Boeisho Kaikaku Kaigi Dai4kai Setsumei Shiryo*, 1 February 2008, http://www.kantei.go.jp/jp/singi/bouei/dai4/pdf/siryou2.pdf; Boeisho, *Dai4kai Boeisho Kaikaku Kaigi Sanko Shiryo*, 1 February 2008, http://www.kantei.go.jp/jp/singi/bouei/dai4/pdf/siryou2.pdf.

12 'Boeicho Amakudari Oi Kigyo Juchu mo Mashi', *Shimbun Akahata*, 12 April 2006, p. 15; Shukan Kinyobihen, *Mitsubishi Juko no Seitai: Kokusaku Boei Kigyo* (Tokyo: Kinyobi, 2008), pp. 26–32.

13 'Kokubozoku no Giin Kyogikai, Beigun Jusangyo to Hinpan ni Kaigo',

Shimbun Akahata, 3 December, http://www.jcp.or.jp/akahta/aik07/2007-12-03/2007120301_02_0.html.

14 Boeisho Kaikaku Kaigi, *Hokokusho: Fuyoji no Bunseki to Kaikaku no Hokosei*, Tokyo, 15 July 2008, http://www.kantei.go.jp/jp/singi/bouei/dai11/pdf/siryou.pdf, pp. 36–40; Boeisho Sogo Shutoku Suishin Purojekkuto Chimu, *Hokokusho*, Tokyo, March 2008, http://www.mod.go.jp/j/info/sougousyutoku/pdf/siryou/10_02.pdf.

15 Boeichohen, *Boei Hakusho 2006* (Tokyo: Okurasho Insatsukyoku, 2006), pp. 276–80; Gen Nakatani, *Daremo Kakenakatta Boeisho no Shinjistu* (Tokyo: Gentosha, 2008).

16 Richard A. Colignon and Chikako Usui, *Amakudari: The Hidden Fabric of Japan's Economy* (Ithaca, NY: Cornell University Press, 2003), pp. 22–3.

17 Boei Kankokai Henshubu, *Boei Nenkan 2007* (Tokyo: Kankokai Henshubu, 2007), p. 329.

18 For the background to the F-SX, see Shinji Otsuki and Masaru Honda, *Nichibei FSX Senso: Nichibei Domei o Yurugasu Gijutsu Masatsu* (Tokyo: Ronsosha, 1991).

19 Reinhard Drifte, *Arms Production in Japan: The Military Applications of Civilian Technology* (Boulder, CO: Westview Press, 1986), pp. 74–8; Oros, *Normalizing Japan*, pp. 94–110.

20 Nihon Keizai Dantai Rengokai Boei Seisan Iinkai, *Waga Kuni Boei Sangyo no Genjo Nado ni Tsuite*, p. 32, presentation provided via personal contact at Keidanren Defense Production Committee, July 2007.

21 Asahi Shimbun Jieitai 50nen Shuzaiha, *Jieitai Shirarezaru Henyo* (Tokyo: Asahi Shimbunsha, 2005), pp. 268–70.

22 METI Boei Sangyo Gijutsu Kiban Kenkyukai, *Boei Sangyo Gijutsu no Iji Ikusei ni Kansuru Kihon-teki Hoko: Niju Isseiki ni okeru Kiban no Kochiku ni Mukete*, Tokyo, November 2000; Boeicho, *Arata na Jidai no Sobi Shutoku o Mezashite: Shin ni Hitsuyo na Boei Seisan Gijutsu Kiban no Kakuritsu ni Mukete*, 2005, p. 1; Boei Kenkyujo, *Waga Kuni no Boei Gijutsu Kiban ga Sobihin Shutoku ni oyabasu Koka ni Kansuru Chosa Kenkyu*, Tokyo, 2006.

23 Junichi Nishiyama, 'Buki Yushutsu to Anzen Hosho', *Kaigai Jijo*, vol. 56, no. 3, 2008, p. 20; Junichi Nishiyama, 'Nihon no Boei to Gijutsu Kaihatsu', in Satoshi Morimoto (ed.), *Kiro ni Tatsu Nihon no Anzen: Anzen Hosho, Kikikanri Seisaku no Jissai to Tenbo* (Tokyo: Hokuseido, 2008), p. 353.

24 Defense Policy Studies Subcommittee, National Defense Division, Policy Research Council, Liberal Democratic Party, *Recommendations on Japan's New Defense Policy: Toward a Safer and More Secure Japan in the World*, 30 March 2003, http://www.jimin.jp/jimin/main/seisaku.html.

25 Nihon Keizai Dantai Rengokai Boei Seisan Iinkai, *Teigen: Kongo no Boeiryoku Seibi no Arikata ni tsuite': Boei Seisan Gijutsu Kiban no Kyoka ni Mukete*, 2004, reported in Nihon Keizai Dantai Rengokai Boei Seisan Iinkai, *Boei Seisan Gijustu Kiban ni Tsuite: Kokunai Kiban no Jujutsu to Kokusai Kyoryoku*, Tokyo, September 2005, p. 6.

26 Abe Shinzo, 'Kaiken de Kosenken mo Mitomeru Beki', *AERA*, 5 August 2004, p. 17.

27 Anzen Hosho to Boeiryokyu ni Kansuru Kondankai, *Anzen Hosho to Boeiryokyu ni Kansuru Kondankai ni Okeru Kore Made no Giron to Gaiyo* 2004, http://www.kantei.go.jp/jp/singi/ampobouei/dai7/7siryou1.pdf, p. 5.

28 'Kensho Buki Yushutsu Sangensoku Kanwa: Kokubozoku, Zaikai ga Kenin', *Asahi Shimbun*, 11 December 2004, p. 4.

29 Boeishohen, *Boei Hakusho 2008* (Tokyo: Zaimusho Insatsukyoku, 2008), p. 388.

30 Armitage and Nye, *The US–Japan Alliance*, p. 29.

31 IFSEC participants are: MHI, IHI, KHI, Shimadzu Corporation, Toshiba, IHI Aerospace, Komatsu, Daikin Industries, NEC, Hitatchi, Fujitsu, MELCO, Boeing, GenCorp Aerojet, GEC, Lockheed Martin, Northrop-Grumman, Raytheon, Science Applications International Cooperation and United Defense.

32 Keidanren/IFSEC, Keidanren, *IFSEC Joint Report: Revised US–Japan Statement of Mutual Interests*, 21 January 2003, http://www.keidanren.or.jp/japanese/policy/2003/005e.html.

33 'Yamada Yoko, Boeizoku Dantai ni Ichiokuen ka, Kyoryokuhi Shishutsu no Bunsho', *Asahi Shimbun*, 30 November 2007, http://www.asahi.com/politics/update/1026/TKY200711300364.html.

34 'Shonin Kammon no Yamada Yoko, Miyazaki Motosenmu "Akiyama-shi Gawa ni Ichiokuen Shishutsu"', *Yomiuri Shimbun*, 22 May 2008, http://www.yomiuri.co.jp/politics/news/20080522-OYT1T00426.htm.

35 The Japanese side included the former JDA Director Generals/Ministers of Defense Tsutomu Kawara, Fumio Kyuma, Fukushiro Nukuga, Tokuichiro Tamazawa, Gen Nakatani, Shigeru Ishiba; former DFAA Director General Noboru Hoshuyama; former DPJ leader Seiji Maehara; former JDA Administrative Vice-Minister Ken Sato; former LDP Secretary-General Tsutomu Takebe; and the Chairman of MHI and senior representatives from MELCO, KHI, NEC, Hitachi, IHI, Toshiba, Itochu, Sumitomo, Marubeni and Yamada Corporation. Former Prime Ministers Abe and Fukuda are also reported to have been members of the board in the past. On the US side, prominent figures included former Secretary of Defense William Cohen, former US Ambassador Michael Armacost and former Pentagon adviser William J. Schneider. Shukan Kinyobihen, *Mitsubishi Juko no Seitai: Kokusaku Boei Kigyo* (Tokyo: Kinyobi, 2008), p. 18.

36 'Kokubo Ugomeku Kane', *Asahi Shimbun*, 25 July 2008, p. 39.

37 Boeishohen, *Boei Hakusho 2008*, p. 388; Kankokai Henshubu, *Boei Nenkan 2006* (Tokyo: Kankokai Henshubu, 2006), pp. 147–8.

38 Kubota Yukari, 'Japan's New Strategy as an Arms Exporter: Revising the Three Principles on Arms Exports', *RIPS Policy Perspectives*, no. 7, November 2008, http://www.rips.or.jp/from_rips/pdf/japans_new_strategy.pdf, pp. 15–16.

Chapter Five

1 Boeishohen, *Boei Hakusho 2007*, p. 285.

2 'Iraku Shien Katsudo Shuryo', *Nihon Keizai Shimbun*, 18 December 2008, p. 2.

3 'Kansha to Fuman: Samawa Kara no Hokoku', *Asahi Shimbun*, 31 August 2008, p. 1; McCormack, *Client State*, p. 70; Maeda Tetsuo, *Jieitai: Henyo no Yukie* (Tokyo: Iwanami Shinsho, 2007), p. 104.

4 For these MSDF figures and full details on its mission in the Indian Ocean up until 2007, see Boeisho, 'Kyu Terotaisaku Tokusoho ni Motozuku Taio Socchi no Kekka ni Tsuite', 1 January 2008, http://www.mod.go.jp/j/news/hokyushien/pdf/siryou_080311.pdf.

5 Pisu Depo, *Chosa Kinkyu Hokoku Kaijikan ga Kyuyu Shita Beikan wa Iraku Sakusen ni Shiyo Shita*, 20 September 2007, http://www.peacedepot.org/media/pcr/mediarelease3/oil.htm.

6 'Kyuyu Giwaku Kuzureru Setsumei: Bei Hitei Seimei, Konkyo Shimesazu', *Asahi Shimbun*, 20 October 2007, p. 4.

7 Boeishohen, *Boei Hakusho 2008*, p. 233.

8 Asahi Shimbun Jieitai 50nen Shuzaiha, *Jieitai Shirarezaru Henyo* (Tokyo: Asahi Shimbunsha, 2005), pp. 52–8.

9 Tetsuo Maeda, *Jieitai: Henyo no Yukie* (Tokyo: Iwanami Shinsho, 2007), pp. 66, 73; 'All GSDF Troops Safely Home from Historic Mission to Iraq', *Japan Times Online*, 26 July 2006, http://search.japantimes.co.jp/cgi-bin/nn20060726f3.html.

10 Kazuhiko Morinaga, 'Indoyo Tsunami no Kyokun', *Securitarian*, March 2005, pp. 3–4; 'Kaijikan, Rikuji Shukueiji ni', *Asahi Shimbun*, 2 February 2005, p. 29.

11 'Sudan PKO Jieitai Haken e Raigetsu ni mo Chosadan', *ibid.*, 15 May 2008, http://www.asahi.com/politics/update/0515/TKY200805150082.html.

12 'Jieitai Haken "Kokyu Hoan Iru" Abe Kanbochokan', *ibid.*, 26 August 2007, p. 3.

13 Ministry of Foreign Affairs Japan, 'Speech by Prime Minister Shinzo Abe at the North Atlantic Council, "Japan and NATO: Toward Further Collaboration"', 12 January 2007, http://www.mofa.go.jp/region/europe/pmv0701/nato.html.

14 'SDF May Head to Afghanistan To Aid Reconstruction', *Japan Times Online*, http://searchjapantimes.co.jp/print/nn20070506a2.html.

15 Ichiro Ozawa, 'Ima Koso Kokusai Anzen Hosho no Gensiku Kakuritsu o', *Sekai*, November 2007, pp. 148–53; 'Afugan Shien "Seiken Toreba Butai Sanka" Ozawashi', *Asahi Shimbun*, 5 October 2008, http://www.asahi.com/politics/update/0105/TKY200801050187.html.

16 'Jieitai Kaigai Katsudo no Ippanhoan, Aki no Rinji Kokkai Teishutsu Shino', *ibid.*, 6 January 2008, http://www.asahi.com/politics/update/1005/TKY200710050157.html; 'Jieitai Kokyu Hoan Kento no Yoto PT Tachiage Jimin Yamasaki', *ibid.*, 10 February 2008, http://www.asahi.com/politics/update/0210/TKY200802100141.html.

17 'Jieitai no Kaigai Haken "Sekkyoku-teki ni" Komura Gaisho', *ibid.*, 6 January 2008, http://www.asahi.com/politics/update/0211/TKY200802110004.html.

18 'Jiteitai Haken Tarinu Kensho: Iraku Senso 5nen Seifu wa Ippanho Suishin', *ibid.*, 20 March 2008, p. 4; 'Afugan Fukkyo e Rikuji Haken, Shusho ga Kento Hyomei', *Yomiuri Shimbun*, 6 January 2008, http://www.

yomiuri.co.jp/politics/news/20080601-OYT1T00432.htm; 'Afugan Fukkyo Shien, Rikugi Haken mo Shino ni Kento Kanboo Chokan', *Asahi Shimbun*, 31 May 2008, http://www.asahi.com/politics/update/0531/TKY200805310288.html; 'Ishiba Boeisho, Jieitai Kaigai Haken Kokyuho no Hitsuyosei Kyocho', *ibid.*, 31 May 2008, http://www.asahi.com/politics/update/0531/TKY200805310175.html; Shigeru Ishiba, 'The Future of East Asian Security', The Seventh IISS Asian Security Summit Shangri-La Dialogue, 31 May 2008, http://www.iiss.org/conferences/the-shangri-la-dialogue/shangri-la-dialogue-2008/plenary-session-speeches-2008/second-plenary-session-the-future-of-east-asian-security/second-plenary-session-shigeru-ishiba; 'Afugan ni Jieitai Heri o, Bei ga Nihon ni Nihon ni Dachin', *Yomiuri Shimbun*, 19 October 2008, http://www.yomiuri.co.jp/politics/news/20081018-OYT1T00700.htm.

19 'Afugan Hondo Haken, Seifu Miokuri Shinho Seiritsu Medo Tatazu', *Asahi Shimbun*, 18 July 2008, http://www.asahi.com/politics/update/0717/TKY200807170309.html.

20 'Afugan de no Taitero Shien, Seifu ga Yusoyo Heri Kaishu ni 40kuen Kyoshutsu', *Yomiuri Shimbun*, 9 January 2009, http://www.yomiuri.co.jp/politics/news/20090109-OYT1T00038.htm.

21 'Aso Motogaisho, Kaiyo Shinpojiumu de Nichi Domei "Saiteigi" o Teigen', *ibid.*, 6 March 2008, http://www.yomiuri.co.jp/politics/news/20080306-OYT1T00346.htm.

22 'Kaizoku Taisaku ni Jieitai Shusho, Somariaoki Haken ni Shinho Kento, *Asahi Shimbun*, 17 October 2008, http://www.asahi.com/politics/update/1017/TKY200810170373.html; 'Somariaoki ni Jieitai Haken, Choto Haken Giren ga Tokusoho o Kento', *Yomiuri Shimbun*, 20 November 2008, http://www.yomiuri.co.jp/politics/news/20081120-OYT1T00612.htm.

23 'Kaiji Haken ni Kabe', *Nihon Keizai Shimbun*, 24 December 2008, p. 2.

24 'Coast Guard To Help MSDF Ships Handle Pirate Arrests off Somalia', *Japan Times Online*, 11 January 2009, http://searchjapantimes.co.jp/print/nn20090111a5.html.

25 'Somariaoki Kaizoku Taisaku, Yoto PT ga Hatsukaigo', *Asahi Shimbun*, 9 January 2009, http://www.asahi.com/politics/update/0109/TKY200901090139.html.

26 'Kaizokusen Shageki o Yonin Yoto PT, Shinho no Kokkoan Ryosho', *ibid.*, 26 February 2009, http://www.asahi.com/politics/update/0225/TKY200902250308.html.

27 'Kaizoku e no Buki Shiyo, Buryoku Koshi ni Atarazu Seifu Kaiken', *ibid.*, 17 December 2008, http://www.asahi.com/politics/update/1217/TKY200812160458.html; 'Kaiji no Buki Shiyo Kengen Kakudai Kaizoku Taisaku Shinho Gaigokusen mo Hogo', *ibid.*, 5 February 2009, http://www.asahi.com/politics/update/0204/TKY200902040314.html.

28 'Seifu, Raigetsu Medo Taisho Yoryo', *Nihon Keizai Shimbun*, 27 December 2008, p. 2; 'Shugekimae mo Shageki Kano ni', *ibid.*, 26 February 2008, p. 1.

29 'Somariaoki Kaizoku Taisaku, Kaiji Goeikan 2seki Haken e', *Yomiuri Shimbun*, 3 February 2009, http://www.yomiuri.co.jp/politics/news/20090203-OYT1T00787.htm; Richard Tanter, 'The Maritime Self-Defence Force Mission in the Indian Ocean: Afghanistan, NATO and Japan's Political Impasse', *Northeast Asia Peace and Security*

Network Policy Forum Online, 4 September 2008, http://www.nautilus.org/fora/security/08068Tanter.html, p. 5

30 'MSDF May Divert Oiler to Somalia Task Force', *Japan Times Online*, 25 February 2009, http://searchjapantimes.co.jp/print/nn20090225a2.html.

31 'Kankoku, Kaiji ni Kyuyu o Dachin Somariaoki de Nihon Kyohi', *Asahi Shimbun*, 22 February 2009, http://www.asahi.com/politics/update/0220/TKY200902200297.html.

32 'Aso, Lee Have Plan To Cooperate on Antipiracy Effort Off Somalia', *Japan Times Online*, 26 January 2009, http://search.japantimes.co.jp/print/nn20090126a1.html.

33 'Kaizoku ni Buki Shiyo Yonin e Seifu no Jieitai Haken Shinhoan', *Asahi Shimbun*, 8 January 2009, http://www.asahi.com/politics/update/0108/TKY200901070296.html.

34 Desmond Ball, 'Whither the Japan–Australia Security Relationship?', *Austral Policy Forum*, 26 September 2006, http://www.nautilus.org/~rmit/forum-reports/0632a-ball.html.

35 Akihiko Tanaka, 'Trilateral Strategic Dialogue: Japan's Perspective', in National Bureau of Asian Research (ed.), *Assessing the Trilateral Strategic Dialogue*, NBR Special Report, no. 16, December 2008, http://www.nbr.org/publications/specialreport/pdf/SR16.pdf, pp. 35–37.

36 Ministry of Foreign Affairs Japan, 'Japan–Australia Joint Declaration on Security Cooperation', 13 March 2007, http://www.mofa.go.jp/region/asia-paci/australia/joint0703.html.

37 Nick Bisley, 'The Japan–Australia Security Declaration and the Changing Regional Security Setting: Wheels, Webs and Beyond?', *Australian Journal of International Affairs*, vol. 61, no. 1, March 2008, pp. 38–52.

38 Ball, 'Whither the Japan–Australia Security Relationship?'.

39 'Kyokuto Joko no Seiyaku Kanwa', *Asahi Shimbun*, 12 November 2004, p. 1.

40 Ministry of Foreign Affairs of Japan, 'Joint Statement of the Security Consultative Committee Alliance Transformation: Advancing United States–Japan Security and Defense Cooperation', 1 May 2007, http://www.mofa.go.jp/region/n-america/us/security/scc/joint0705.html.

41 'Beigun no Igisukan 5seki, Nihon Shuhen ni Tenkai', *Yomiuri Shimbun*, 26 March 2009, http://www.yomiuri.co.jp/politics/news/20090326-OYT1T0017.htm.

42 'Schieffer's Call for Missile Defense Help Raises Constitution Issue', *Japan Times Online*, 28 October 2006, http://search.japantimes.co.jp/print/nn20061028a7.html;'Collective Defense Ban Crazy: Lawless', *ibid.*, 7 December 2006, http://search.japantimes.co.jp/print/nn.20061207a3.html; 'US Calls on Japan To Shield It From Missiles', *ibid.*, 17 May 2007, http://search.japantimes.co.jp/print/nn20070517a2.html.

43 'Japan, US Vow Tighter Military, Security Ties', *ibid.*, 2 May 2007, http://search.japantimes.co.jp/print/nn20070502a2.html; 'Nichibei, Gunji Himitsu Hogo e Kyotei 2 Purasu 2 de Goi', *Asahi Shimbun*, 2 May 2007, http://www.asahi.com/politics/update/0501/TKY200705010443.html.

44 'Senryaku Buntan Nao Futomei', *ibid.*, 2 May 2006, p. 4.

45 'Abe's Gov't Downplays Yet Another Minister Remark on US Policy', *Kyodo News on Yahoo! News Asia*, 5 February 2007, http://asia.news.yahoo.com/070205/kyodo/d8n3i1080.html.

46 'Japan, the US Clarify Rules on Handling Secret Data', *Japan Times Online*, 11 August 2007, http://searchjapantimes.co.jp/print/nn20070811a5.html.

47 'Chosen Yuji no Nichibei Sakusen, Ryoseifu Bappon Minaoshi ni Chakute', *Yomiuri Shimbun*, 11 November 2008, http://www.yomiuri.co.jp/politics/news/20081110-OYT1T00720.htm.

Chapter 6

1 Sabine Frühstück, *Uneasy Warriors: Gender, Memory, and Popular Culture in the Japanese Army* (Berkeley, CA: University of California Press, 2007), p. 24.

2 *Ibid.*

3 *Ibid.*, pp. 128–38; Sabine Frühstück and Eyal ben Ari, '"Now We Show It All!" Normalization and the Management of Violence in Japan's Armed Forces', *Journal of Japanese Studies*, vol. 28, no. 1, 2002, pp. 1–39.

4 Boeichohen, *Boei Hakusho 2004* (Tokyo: Zaimusho Insatsukyoku, 2004), p. 309; 'Boeisho ga Pairoto Joken Kanwa, Akuryoku Sanju Kiro Miman, Megane OK', *Yomiuri Shimbun*, 11 August 2008, http://www.yomiuri.co.jp/national/news/20080811-OYT1T00473.htm; 'MSDF Women To Serve on Ships', *Japan Times*, 26 September 2008, http://search.japantimes.co.jp/print/nn20080926f4.html.

5 Frühstück, *Uneasy Warriors*, pp. 36–9.

6 John Endicott, *Japan's Nuclear Option: Political, Technical and Strategic Factors* (New York: Praeger, 1975).

7 'Jimin Seichokai "Kaku Hoyu no Giron Hitsuyo" Shusho wa Sangensoku o Kyocho', *Asahi Shimbun*, 15 October 2006, http://www.asahi.com/special/nuclear/TKY200610150124.html.

8 'Kaku Hoyu "Giron wa Daiji" Aso Gaisho, Kokkai de Hatsugen', *ibid.*, 19 October 2006, http://www.asahi.com/special/nuclear/TKY200610180447.html; 'Aso Gaisho, 'Kaku Hoyu Giron Fusatsu Shinai', *ibid.*, 19 October 2006, http://www.asahi.com/special/nuclear/TKY200610180297.html; *Kokkai Shugiin Kaigiroku Gaimuiinkai*, 2go, 25 October 2006, p. 112, available at http://kokkai.ndl.go.jp.

9 'Nakagawashi, Bei de no Jizetsu de "Kaku Giron", Futatabi Yoto Fukai', *Asahi Shimbun*, 28 October 2006, http://www.asahi.com/special/nuclear/TKY200610280290.html.

10 'Kim Diabetic, May Nuke Japan, Nakagawa Says', *Japan Times Online*, 21 October 2006, http://search.japantimes.co.jp/cgi-bin/nn20061021a4.html.

11 'Abe Affirms that Japan Will Still Shun Nuclear Weapons', *ibid.*, 17 October 2006, http://search.japantimes.co.jp/cgi-bin/nn20061017a8.html; 'Aso Keen To Explore Nukes, But Abe Says Debate Is "Finished"', *Japan Times Online*, 19 October 2006, http://search.japantimes.co.jp/print/nn20061109a2.html.

12 'Abe Says No to Nukes But Allows Discussion', *ibid.*, 9 November 2006, http://search.japantimes.co.jp/cgi-bin/nn20061109a2.html; *Kokkai Shugiin Kaigiroku Kokka Kihon Seisaku Iinkai Godo Chosakai*, 2go, 8 November 2006, pp. 13–15, available at http://kokkai.ndl.go.jp.

13 'Cabinet To Cease Talking about Nukes, Abe Says', *Japan Times Online*, 21 November 2006, http://search.japantimes.co.jp/print/nn20061121b2.html.

14 'Nihon no Kaku Busoron, Chugoku mo Kennen Busshu Daitoryo ga Hanno', *Asahi Shimbun*, 17 October 2006, http://www.asahi.com/special/nuclear/TKY200610170272.html.

15 'No Japan Nukes: Rice', *Japan Times Online*, 12 October 2006, http://search.japantimes.co.jp/print/nn20061015a2.html.

16 Jim Lobe, 'US Neo-Conservatives Call for Japanese Nukes, Regime Change in North Korea', *Japan Focus*, 17 October 2006, http://japanfocus.org/products/details/2249. For an earlier articulation of the strategy of pushing Japan towards nuclearisation to counter North Korea, see Ted Galen Carpenter, 'Options for Dealing with North Korea', *Foreign Policy Briefing*, no. 73, 6 January 2003, http://www.cato.org/pubs/fpbriefs/fpb73.pdf. For a discussion of the 'Japan Card' strategy in general, see Kurt M. Campbell and Tsuyoshi Sunohara, 'Japan: Thinking the Unthinkable', in Kurt M. Campbell, Robert J. Einhorn and Mitchell B. Reiss (eds), *The Nuclear Tipping Point: Why States Reconsider Their Nuclear Choices* (Washington DC: Brookings Institution Press, 2005), p. 246.

17 'Wen Lauds Abe's Non-Nuclear Stand', *Japan Times Online*, 25 October 2006, http://search.japantimes.co.jp/print/nn20061024a5.html.

18 'Japan Talk of Nukes "Not Desirable": Ban', *Japan Times Online*, 7 November 2006, http://search.japantimes.co.jp/cgi-bin/nn20061107a1.html.

19 Tetsuo Maeda and Shigeaki Ijima, *Kokkai Shingi kara Boeiron Yomitoku* (Tokyo: Sanseido, 2003), p. 72.

20 Campbell and Sunohara, 'Japan: Thinking the Unthinkable', p. 223.

21 Katsuhisa Furukawa, 'Nuclear Option, Arms Control, and Extended Deterrence: In Search of a New Framework for Japan's Nuclear Policy', in Benjamin L. Self and Jeffrey W. Thompson (eds), *Japan's Nuclear Option: Security, Politics and Policy in the 21st Century* (Washington DC: Henry L. Stimson Center, 2003), pp. 104–5.

22 Yuri Kase, 'The Costs and Benefits of Japan's Nuclearization: An Insight into the 1968/1970 Internal Report', *Non-Proliferation Review*, vol. 8, no. 2, Summer 2001, pp. 55–68; Llewelyn Hughes, 'Why Japan Will Not Go Nuclear (Yet): International and Domestic Constraints on the Nuclearization of Japan', *International Security*, vol. 31, no. 4, Spring 2007, pp. 77–80.

23 International Panel on Fissile Materials, *Global Fissile Material Report 2007* (Princeton, NJ: Program on Science and Global Security, 2007), http://www.fissilematerials.org/ipfm/site_down/gfmr07.pdf; Eichi Katahara, 'Japan's Plutonium Policy: Consequences for Non Proliferation', *The Non-Proliferation Review*, vol. 5, no. 1, Autumn 1997, p. 59.

24 'Japan Can Be a Nuclear Power: Ozawa', *Japan Times Online*, 7 April 2002, http://search.japantimes.co.jp/cgi-bin/nn20020407a1.html.

25 'Non-nuclear Policy To Stay As Is: Koizumi', *ibid.*, 13 June 2002, http://search.japantimes.co.jp/cgi-bin/nn20020613a6.html.

26 Terumasa Nakanishi, 'Nihon Kaku Buso e no Ketsudan', *Shokun*, August 2003, pp. 22–33; Terumasa Nakanishi, 'Nuclear Weapons for Japan', *Japan Echo*, vol. 30, no. 5, October 2003, pp. 48–54;

Terumasa Nakanishi (ed.), *Nihon Kaku Buso no Ronten: Kokka Sonritsu no Kiki Ikinuku Michi* (Tokyo: PHP Kenkyusho, 2006); Hajime Izumi and Katsuhisa Furukawa, 'Not Going Nuclear: Japan's Response to North Korea's Nuclear Test', *Arms Control Today*, vol. 37, no. 6, June 2007, http://www.arms control.org/act/2007_06/CoverStory.

27 IIPS, *21seiki no Nihon no Kokkazo ni Tsuite*, 5 September 2006, http://www.iips.org/kokkazouh.pdf; IIPS, *Sanko Hosoku Setsumei*, 5 September 2006, http://www.iips.org/kokkazoua.pdf.

28 Shigeru Ishiba, 'Koshi Ishiba Maeboeichokan', in Buntaro Kuroi (ed.), *Nihon no Boei Nanatsu no Ronten* (Tokyo: Takarajimasha, 2005), pp. 51–2; Mike M. Mochizuki, 'Japan Tests the Nuclear Taboo', *Non-Proliferation Review*, vol. 14, no. 2, July 2007, p. 318; Jun Sakurada, 'The Folly of Calls for Nuclear Armament', *Japan Echo*, vol. 30, no. 4, August 2003, pp. 42–3.

29 'Junko Missairu "Tomahoku" Kento o Nukuga-shi Beikoku de Koen', *Asahi Shimbun*, 2 May 2007, http://www.asahi.com/politics/update/0502/TKY200705020251.html; Fukushiro Nukaga, 'Nihon no Boei Seisaku to Nichibei Kyoryoku', Paper Presented at Ninth Japan–US Security Strategy Conference, Heritage Foundation, Washington DC, 1 May 2007, http://www.ja-cpce.jp/conf_US2007-nukaga1.pdf, p. 2.

30 Tokyo Zaidan Seisaku Kenkyubu, *Atarashii Nihon no Anzen Hosho Senryaku: Taso Kyochoteki Anzen Hosho*, Tokyo, 8 October 2008, pp. 9, 22.

31 'Nichibei no Renkei Kyoka o Kakunin Abe Shusho, Raisu Chokan to Kaidan', *Asahi Shimbun*, 19 October 2006, http://www.asahi.com/special/nuclear/TKY200610190232.html.

32 Ryuichi Teshima, 'Amerika wa Kaku no Kasa o Kakuyaku Shita: Gaimu Daijin Dokusen Intabyu', *Chuo Koron*, December 2006, p. 55.

33 'National Security Debate Mushrooming Since Oct 9', *Japan Times Online*, 25 November 2006, http://search.japantimes.co.jp/mail/nn20061125a2.html.

34 Emma Chanlett-Avery and Mary Beth Nikitin, *Japan's Nuclear Future: Policy Debate, Prospects and US Interests, CRS Report for Congress*, 9 May 2008, Washington DC, p. 8; Shigeru Ishiba, *Kokubo* (Tokyo: Shinshosha, 2005), p. 145; Mochizuki, 'Japan Tests the Nuclear Taboo', p. 309.

35 'Talk of Going Nuclear Irks Opposition', *Japan Times*, 3 November 2006, http://search.japantimes.co.jp/cgi-bin/nn20061103a7.html.

36 'Aso Should Be Axed for Nuke Comments', *ibid.*, 10 November 2006, http://search.japantimes.co.jp/cgi-bin/nn20061110a6.html.

37 'LDP, Komeito Officials Seek To Rein in Nuke Talk', *ibid.*, 6 November 2006, http://search.japantimes.co.jp/cgi-bin/nn20061106a1.html.

38 'A-bombings "Couldn't Be Helped": Kyuma', *ibid.*, 1 July 2007, http://search.japantimes.co.jp/cgi-bin/nn20070701a1.html.

39 Matake Kamiya, 'Nuclear Japan: Oxymoron or Coming Soon?', *Washington Quarterly*, vol. 26, no. 1, Winter 2002–2003, p. 66; Mochizuki, 'Japan Tests the Nuclear Taboo', p. 307.

40 Jeffrey W. Thompson and Benjamin L. Self, 'Nuclear Energy, Space Launch Vehicles and Advanced Technology: Japan's Prospects for Nuclear Breakout', in Benjamin L. Self and Jeffrey W. Thompson (eds), *Japan's*

Nuclear Option: Security, Politics and Policy in the 21st Century (Washington DC: Henry L. Stimson Center, 2003), pp. 162–6; Kensuke Ebata, 'Kaku ni Muchi na Nihonjin ni Okuru Kiso Chishiki', *Chuo Koron*, December 2006, pp. 49–51.

41 Shinichi Kitaoka, 'Kita no Kaku o Yokushi Suru Tame no Ttsutsu no Sentakushi', *ibid.*, December 2006, pp. 39–40.

42 Brad Glosserman, 'Straight Talk about Japan's Nuclear Option', *PacNet Newsletter*, 11 October 2006, http://www.csis.org/component/option,com_csis_pubs/task,view/id,3532/type,3.

43 Izumi and Furukawa, 'Not Going Nuclear'.

44 Terumasa Nakanishi, 'Nihon Kaku Buso e no Ketsudan', *Shokun*, August 2003, p. 31; Ebata, 'Kaku ni Muchi na Nihonjin ni Okuru Kiso Chishiki', pp. 48–9.

45 This type of strategy was advocated by Takuya Kubo, the director of the Defense Policy Bureau of the JDA in the 1970s and a key framer of the 1976 NDPO. Kubo argued: 'If Japan increases its peaceful nuclear capability in such a way as to enable significant nuclear armament at anytime (which is probably already the case), the United States, fearing the impact on instability brought about by nuclear proliferation, would seek to maintain its nuclear guarantee to Japan'. Takuya Kubo, *Boeiryoku Seibi no Kangatekata (KB Kojin Ronbun)*, Detabesu Sekai to Nihon, Sengo Nihon Seiji-Kokusai Kankei Detabesu, 29 February 2001, http://www.ioc.u-tokyo.ac.jp/~worldjpn/documents/texts/JPSC/19710220.O1J.html. For a similar view, see Izumi and Furukawa, 'Not Going Nuclear: Japan's Response to North Korea's Nuclear Test'.

46 Tomohito Shinoda, 'Taigai Seisaku Kettei no Akuta Toshite no Ozawa Ichiro', in Kohei Hashimoto (ed.), *Nihon Gaiko Seisaku Kettei Yoin* (Tokyo: PHP Kenkyujo, 1999), p. 41.

47 Yoshitaka Sasaki, *Umi o Wataru Jietai* (Tokyo: Iwanami Shinsho, 1992), pp. 13–17; Nobumasa Tanaka, *Kempo Kyujo no Sengoshi* (Tokyo: Iwanami Shinsho, 2005), p. 135; Akihiko Tanaka, 'The Domestic Context: Japanese Politics and UN Peacekeeping', in Selig S. Harrison and Masashi Nishihara (eds), *UN Peacekeeping: Japanese and American Perspectives* (New York: Carnegie Endowment for International Peace, 1995), pp. 93–4.

48 Shigenobu Tamura, *Kempo to Anzen Hosho* (Tokyo: Nansosha, 1993), pp. 101–35.

49 'Press Conference by Prime Minister Junichiro Koizumi: The Basic Plan Regarding the Measures Based on the Law Concerning the Special Measures on Humanitarian and Reconstruction Assistance in Iraq', 9 December 2003, http://www.kantei.go.jp/foreign/koizumispeech/2003/12/09press_e.html.

50 'Hokyuchu, Beikansen ga Kogeki Uketara, "Kobetsu Jieiken de Osen"', *Asahi Shimbun*, 18 October 2008, p. 4.; Michael Auslin and Christopher Griffin, *Securing Freedom: The US–Japan Alliance in a New Era* (Washington DC: American Enterprise Institute, 2008), p. 25, http://www.aei.org/docLib/20081118_SecuringFreedom.pdf.

51 'Statement of the Chief Cabinet Secretary of Japan on the Cabinet Decision "On the Introduction of Ballistic Missile Defense System and

Other Measures"', Ministry of Defense of Japan, *Defense of Japan 2007* (Tokyo: Intergroup, 2007), p. 500.

52 Satoshi Morimoto and Sugio Takahashi, 'BMD to Nihon no Boei Seisaku', in Satoshi Morimoto (ed.), *Misairu Boei: Atarashii Kokusai Anzen Hosho no Kozu* (Tokyo: Nihon Kokusai Mondai Kenkyujo, 2002), pp. 308–9.

53 'Kyuma Chokan Kaiken Gaiyo', 21 November 2006, Ministry of Defense of Japan, pp. 1–3, http://www.mod.go.jp/j/kisha/2006/11/21.pdf; 'Takoku e Mukau Missairu Yogeki "Jissai ni wa Muri" Kyuma Chokan', *Asahi Shimbun*, 21 November 2006, http://www.asahi.com/politics/update/1121/002.html.

54 'US Calls On Japan To Shield It From Missiles'.

55 'Shudan-teki Jieiken Shomen Kara Giron o: Bei Hyoteki no Missairu Yogeki Kenkyu', *Yomiuri Shimbun*, 24 November 2006, p. 11.

56 *Asahi Shimbun Yukan*, 5 October 2001, p. 17.

57 Shugiin Kempo Chosakai, *Shugiin Kempo Chosakai Hokokusho*, April 2005, http://www.shugiin.go.jp/index.nsf/html/index_kenpou.htm, pp. 301–306; 'Shugiin Kempo Chosa Saishu Hokoku' *Yomiuri Shimbun*, 16 April 2005, p. 13.

58 Sangiin Kempo Chosakai, Nipponkoku Kempo ni Kansuru Chosa Hokokusho, April 2005, http://www.sangiin.go.jp/japanese/kenpou/houkokusyo/pdf/honhoukoku.pdf, pp. 66–102.

59 Defense Policy Studies Subcommittee, National Defense Division, Policy Research Council, Liberal Democratic Party, *Recommendations on Japan's New Defense Policy –Towards a Safer and More Secure Japan and the World*, 30 March 2004, pp. 8–9, http://www.jimin.jp/jimin/seisaku/2004/seisaku-006.html.

60 Jiyu Minshuto, *Shinkempo Soan*, 22 Novmember 2005, pp. 2, 4–5. http://www.jimin.jp/jimin/shin_kenpou/shiryou/pdf/051122_a.pdf.

61 'Jimin Shinkempo Kiso Yoko', *Asahi Shimbun*, 5 April 2005, p. 1.

62 'Jieitai o Do Suru Kanzen Shimureshon', *AERA*, 5 August 2004, p. 19.

63 Richard J. Samuels, *Politics, Security Policy and Japan's Cabinet Legislation Bureau*, Japan Policy Research Institute Working Paper No. 99, March 2004, pp. 7–12.

64 Patrick Köllner, 'Factionalism in Japanese Political Parties Revisited or How Do Factions in the LDP and DPJ Differ', *Japan Forum*, vol. 16, no. 1, 2004, pp. 96–9.

65 'Minshu Anzen Hosho no Kabe', *Asahi Shimbun*, 4 August 2004, p. 4.

66 'DPJ Set To Submit Own Proposals on Constitution', *Japan Times Online*, 14 January 2004, http://search.japantimes.co.jp/member/member.html?appURL=nn20040114a1.html.

67 'Minshu Riberarusei Kesshu', *Asahi Shimbun*, 8 February 2006, p. 4.

68 Katsuya Okada, 'Atarashii Nihon to 21seiki no Nichibei Kankei', 29 July 2004, http://www.dpj.or.jp/seisaku/unei/BOX_UN0178.html.

69 'Maehara Backs Changing War-Renouncing Article 9', *Japan Times Online*, 18 October 2005, http://www.japantimes.co.jp/cgi-bin/getarticle.pl5?nn20051018a6.htm.

70 'Minshu Riberarusei Kesshu', p. 4.

71 Minshuto Kempo Chosakai, *Minshuto Kempo Teigen*, 31 October 2005, pp. 15–16.

72 Shinzo Abe, *Utsukushii Kuni E* (Tokyo: Bunshun Shinsho, 2006), pp. 121–32; 'Hoshu Saikikochiku Direnma', *Asahi Shimbun*, 29 August 2006, p. 4.

73 'Jimin "Taiko wa Sakusei Kanno":

Kaiken Genan Shingi no Toketsu Kikan', *ibid.*, 27 April 2007, p. 1.

74 'Shudan-teki Jieiken Kenkyu, Getsunai ni mo Yushikisha Kaigi Secchi', *Nihon Keizai Shimbun Yukan*, 5 April 2007, p. 2.

75 'Missairu Boeo, Kako no Kanbo Chokan Danwa Minaoshi o Shisa Shiozaki-shi', *Asahi Shimbun*, 20 November 2006, http://www.asahi.com/politics/update/1120/011.html; 'Missile Shield Policy May Be Reviewed', *Japan Times Online*, 21 November 2006, http://www.japantimes.co.jp/print /nn20061121a1.html.

76 'Shudan-teki Jieiken Kondankai Menbā: Sekkyokuha Zurari Shusho Yori', *Asahi Shimbun*, 26 April 2007, p. 4.

77 Anzen Hosho no Ho-teki Kiban no Saikochiku ni Kansuru Kondankai, *Anzen Hosho no Ho-teki Kiban no Saikochiku ni Kansuru Kondankai Hokokusho*, 24 June 2008, http://www.kantei.go.jp/jp/singi/anzenhosyou/houkokusho.pdf, pp. 9–10.

78 *Ibid.*, pp. 11–12, 22.

79 *Ibid.*, pp. 13–16.

80 *Ibid.*, p. 23.

81 For the full deliberations of the panel, see *Anzen Hosho no Ho-teki Kiban no Saikochiku ni Kansuru Kondankai*, http://www.kantei.go.jp/jp/singi/anzenhosyou/index.html.

82 Kokumin Tohyo Hoan Shuin Tsuka Mokuzen Seikyoku ni', *Asahi Shimbun*, 10 April 2008, p. 2.

83 'Shudan-teki Jieiken Kondankai Menbā: Sekkyokuha Zurari Shusho Yori', *ibid.*, 26 April 2007, p. 4; 'Ota Says No Way to "Collective Self-Defense"', *Japan Times*, 3 May 2007, http://search.japantimes.co.jp/print/nn20070503f4.html.

84 'Shudan-teki Jieiken Kenkyu Yamasaki Taku-shira ga Kennen', *Asahi Shimbun*, 27 April 2007, p. 4; 'Shudan-teki Jieiken Kondankai Menbā: Sekkyokuha Zurari Shusho Yori', *ibid.*, 26 April 2007, p. 4.

85 'Shudan-teki Jieiken no Rongi Shissoku, Shusho Hiyayaka, Hoseikon Makuhiki', *ibid.*, 26 June 2008, http://www.asahi.com/politics/update/0625/TKY200806250006.html.

86 'Aso Raises Collective Self-Defense', *Japan Times*, 2 October 2008, http://search.japantimes.co.jp/print/nn20081002f1.html.

87 'Shudan-teki Jieiken no Seifu Kenkai, Gaisho, Boeisho "Jurai Dori"', *Asahi Shimbun*, 1 October 2008, http://www.asahi.com/politics/update/1001/TKY200809300429.html.

88 'Aso Backtracks on Collective Defense', *Japan Times*, 5 November 2008, http://search.japantimes.co.jp/print/nn20081105a3.html.

89 'Public Gradually More Accepting of Constitutional Change', *ibid.*, 4 May 2004, http://search.japantimes.co.jp/print/nn20040503a3.html.

90 'Ryudoka Suru Goken, Kaiken', *Asahi Shimbun*, 3 May 2006, p. 1; 'Kaiken Nijimu Genjitsu Shiko', *ibid.*, 3 May 2006, p. 10.

91 'Kenpo 60nen Shazetsu no Hyoka wa', *ibid.*, 27 May 2007, p. 4; '78% Say Article 9 Has Helped Keep Japan Peace', *ibid.*, 3 May 2007, http://www.asahi.com/english/Herald-asahi/TKY200705030084.html.

92 'Poll: 66% Want Article 9 To Stay As Is', *ibid.*, 5 May 2008, http://www.asahi.com/english/Herald-asahi/TKY200805050052.html; Paul Midford, 'Japan: Balancing Between a Hegemon and Would-Be Hegemon', unpublished paper presented at Stockholm Workshop on Japanese Political Economy, Stockholm, Sweden, 13–14 June 2008, p. 29.

93 'Kenpo Honsha Yoron Chosa', *Yomiuri Shimbun*, 4 April 2006, p. 14; 'Kenpo 60nen Shazetsu no Hyoka wa', *Asahi Shimbun*, 27 May 2007, p. 4.

94 *Atarashii Nihon no Anzen Hosho Senryaku: Taso Kyocho-teki Anzen Hosho Senryaku*, Tokyo, Tokyo Zaidan, 8 October 2008, p. 25, http://www.tkfd.or.jp/admin/files/081008.pdf.

95 Boeicho, *Manga de Yomu! Boei Hakusho 2005* (Tokyo: Zaidan Hojin Boei Kyosaikai, 2005).

96 Boeisho, *Manga de Wakaru! Nihon no Boei: Dando Missairu kara Nihon o Mamoru* (Tokyo: Jiji Gappo, 2007).

97 Shigeru Ishiba, *Kokubo* (Tokyo: Shinshosha, 2005); Shigeru Ishiba, *Manga de Yomu Kokubo Nyumon* (Tokyo: Aoba Shuppan, 2007).

98 For examples of these publications, see Bessatsu Takarajima, *Jieitai vs Chugokugun* (Tokyo: Bessatsu Takarajima, 2005); Bessatsu Takarajima, *Jieitai Shinsedai Heiki Perfect Book 2008* (Tokyo: Bessatsu Takarajima); and Goto Noriyuki, *Sono Toki Jieitai wa Nihon o Mamoreru no Ka?* (Tokyo: Futabasha, 2008).

99 Jiyu Minshuto, *Shinkenpo Soan*, 28 October2005,http://www.kenpoukaigi.gr.jp/seitoutou/051028jimin-sinkenpousouan.pdf.

100 MEXT, *Kyoiku Kihon Hoan, Shinkyu Taisho Hyomokuji*, http://www.mext.go.jp/b_menu/houan/an/06042712/005.pdf.

101 McCormack, *Client State*, p. 150.

102 Carol Gluck, *Japan's Modern Myths: Ideology in the Late Meiji Period* (Princeton, NJ: Princeton University Press, 1985), p. 121.

103 Paul Midford, 'Japanese Mass Opinion Toward the War on Terrorism', in Robert D. Eldridge and Paul Midford (eds), *Japanese Public Opinion and the War on Terrorism* (New York: Palgrave Macmillan, 2008), pp. 15–18.

104 *Ibid.*, pp. 32–5.

Conclusion

1 Armitage and Nye, *The US–Japan Alliance*, pp. 21–2.

2 'Zainichi Beigun Shukusho Kishimu Yato', *Nihon Keizai Shimbun*, 27 February 2009, p. 2.

3 INSS, *The United States and Japan: Advancing Toward a Mature Partnership INSS Speical Report*, October 2000, http://www.ndu.edu/inss/strforum/SR_01/SR_Japan.htm.

Adelphi books are published eight times a year by Routledge Journals, an imprint of Taylor & Francis, 4 Park Square, Milton Park, Abingdon, Oxfordshire OX14 4RN, UK.

A subscription to the institution print edition, ISSN 0567-932X, includes free access for any number of concurrent users across a local area network to the online edition, ISSN 1478-5145.

2009 Annual Adelphi Subscription Rates		
Institution	£381	$669 USD
Individual	£222	$378 USD
Online only	£361	$636 USD

Dollar rates apply to subscribers in all countries except the UK and the Republic of Ireland where the pound sterling price applies. All subscriptions are payable in advance and all rates include postage. Journals are sent by air to the USA, Canada, Mexico, India, Japan and Australasia. Subscriptions are entered on an annual basis, i.e. January to December. Payment may be made by sterling cheque, dollar cheque, international money order, National Giro, or credit card (Amex, Visa, Mastercard).

For more information, visit our website: **http://www.informaworld.com/adelphipapers.**

For a complete and up-to-date guide to Taylor & Francis journals and books publishing programmes, and details of advertising in our journals, visit our website: **http://www.informaworld.com.**

Ordering information:
USA/Canada: Taylor & Francis Inc., Journals Department, 325 Chestnut Street, 8th Floor, Philadelphia, PA 19106, USA. **UK/Europe/Rest of World:** Routledge Journals, T&F Customer Services, T&F Informa UK Ltd., Sheepen Place, Colchester, Essex, CO3 3LP, UK.

Advertising enquiries to:
USA/Canada: The Advertising Manager, Taylor & Francis Inc., 325 Chestnut Street, 8th Floor, Philadelphia, PA 19106, USA. Tel: +1 (800) 354 1420. Fax: +1 (215) 625 2940.

UK/Europe/Rest of World: The Advertising Manager, Routledge Journals, Taylor & Francis, 4 Park Square, Milton Park, Abingdon, Oxfordshire OX14 4RN, UK. Tel: +44 (0) 20 7017 6000. Fax: +44 (0) 20 7017 6336.

The print edition of this journal is printed on ANSI conforming acid-free paper by Bell & Bain, Glasgow, UK.

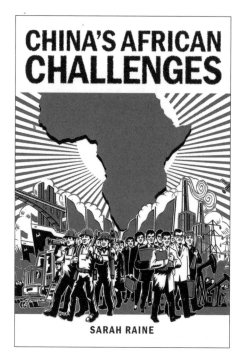